Reading Achievement
Comprehension Activities to Promote Essential Reading Skills

Grade 1

by
Alison Shelton

Table of Contents

Introduction

Welcome to the **Reading Achievement** series! Each book in this series is designed to reinforce the reading skills appropriate for each grade level and to encourage high-level thinking skills. Because reading is an essential part of all disciplines, mastery of these skills can help students succeed in all academic areas. In addition, experiencing success in reading can increase a student's self-esteem and motivate him or her to read more, both in and out of the classroom.

Each **Reading Achievement** book offers challenging questions for students to answer in response to a variety of grade-level appropriate passages. Various types of reading passages are represented in this book, including fiction, nonfiction, letters, and word searches. The format and questions are similar to those found on standardized reading tests. The experience students gain from answering questions in this format may help increase their test scores. In addition, these exercises can be used to enhance your school-adopted reading program, to individualize instruction, to provide extra practice for home schoolers, or to review skills between grades.

Each **Reading Achievement** book contains additional features to enhance usability. Four pretests, in standardized test format, have been included at the beginning of each book. The pretests have been designed so that they may be used individually, as four stand-alone tests, or in groups. Another convenient feature is a scoring box on each activity page. This scoring box can be programmed to suit your specific classroom and student needs with total problems, total correct, and score.

The following reading skills are covered within this book:

- **comprehension**
- **phonics**
- **sequencing**
- **true or false**
- **vocabulary**

Read the story below.

Duncan and his family went to the beach. They played in the sand and built sand castles. They swam in the ocean and played in the waves. They walked along the beach and collected seashells. When it was time to go home, they were sad to leave the seaside.

Answer the questions. Fill in the circle beside the correct answer.

1. Where did Duncan and his family go on their vacation?
   - ○ the beach
   - ○ the mountains
   - ○ to visit Duncan's aunt

2. Which of these did Duncan not do at the beach?
   - ○ build sand castles
   - ○ collect shells
   - ○ fly kites

3. In the last sentence, the word "seaside" means the same as:
   - ○ house
   - ○ beach
   - ○ city

4. How did Duncan feel when it was time to go home?
   - ○ sad   ○ happy   ○ scared

4

Total Problems:	Total Correct:	Score:

Name _____

Read the story below.

Bam! Bam! What was that noise? Mother ran to see. So did Ben and Sam. It was just their baby brother. He was on the floor with the pots and pans and spoons.

Answer the questions. Fill in the circle beside the correct answer.

1. From this story, you can tell that:
   ○ Three people ran.
   ○ No one cared about the noise.
   ○ Mother took the pots and pans away.

2. Which word rhymes with "Bam" and "Sam"?
   ○ him
   ○ home
   ○ ham

3. In this story, the baby is probably in the:
   ○ yard
   ○ living room
   ○ kitchen

4. Who was making the noise they heard?
   ○ the dog
   ○ the baby
   ○ Father

Total Problems:	Total Correct:	Score:

Read the story below.

    Dogs do many funny things. For example, when they get wet, they like to wait until we are standing right beside them, and then they shake water all over us! Why do they do this? We really don't know. Some people say that dogs really do not like being wet, and this is their way of telling us. Another idea is that they are having so much fun, they want to share it with us!

Answer the questions. Fill in the circle beside the correct answer, or write the answer on the lines provided.

1. This story is about:
   ○ why dogs shake water on us
   ○ giving a dog a bath
   ○ why dogs are funny

2. What might be one reason that dogs shake water on us?
   ○ They want to share the fun.
   ○ We are standing too close to them.
   ○ They don't have a towel.

3. Why do you think that dogs shake water on us?

_____

_____

Total Problems: Total Correct: Score:

Read the story below.

Brandon had been fishing all morning. He had not caught any fish, and he was hungry. "I am going to get something to eat," he said. Brandon walked away. His little sister Michelle came over and picked up Brandon's fishing pole. Suddenly, it bent. A fish! Michelle pulled in a big fish. When Brandon came back, he was sorry he had left his pole.

Answer the questions. Fill in the circle beside the correct answer.

1. Why did Brandon leave his fishing pole?
   ○ He was sleepy.
   ○ He was hungry.
   ○ It was broken.

2. How long had Brandon been fishing?
   ○ all afternoon
   ○ all day
   ○ all morning

3. When Michelle picked up Brandon's fishing pole, it:
   ○ bent
   ○ fell in the water
   ○ broke

Total Problems:	Total Correct:	Score:

Name _____   Pretest

Read the story below.

Duncan and his family went to the beach. They played in the sand and built sand castles. They swam in the ocean and played in the waves. They walked along the beach and collected seashells. When it was time to go home, they were sad to leave the seaside.

Answer the questions. Fill in the circle beside the correct answer.

1. Where did Duncan and his family go on their vacation?
   - ● the beach
   - ○ the mountains
   - ○ to visit Duncan's aunt

2. Which of these did Duncan not do at the beach?
   - ○ build sand castles
   - ○ collect shells
   - ● fly kites

3. In the last sentence, the word "seaside" means the same as:
   - ○ house
   - ● beach
   - ○ city

4. How did Duncan feel when it was time to go home?
   - ● sad   ○ happy   ○ scared

(4) | Total Problems: | Total Correct: | Score: | © Carson-Dellosa CD-2200

Name _____   Pretest

Read the story below.

Bam! Bam! What was that noise? Mother ran to see. So did Ben and Sam. It was just their baby brother. He was on the floor with the pots and pans and spoons.

Answer the questions. Fill in the circle beside the correct answer.

1. From this story, you can tell that:
   - ● Three people ran.
   - ○ No one cared about the noise.
   - ○ Mother took the pots and pans away.

2. Which word rhymes with "Bam" and "Sam"?
   - ○ him
   - ○ home
   - ● ham

3. In this story, the baby is probably in the:
   - ○ yard
   - ○ living room
   - ● kitchen

4. Who was making the noise they heard?
   - ○ the dog
   - ● the baby
   - ○ Father

© Carson-Dellosa CD-2200 | Total Problems: | Total Correct: | Score: | (5)

Name _____   Pretest

Read the story below.

Dogs do many funny things. For example, when they get wet, they like to wait until we are standing right beside them, and then they shake water all over us! Why do they do this? We really don't know. Some people say that dogs really do not like being wet, and this is their way of telling us. Another idea is that they are having so much fun, they want to share it with us!

Answer the questions. Fill in the circle beside the correct answer, or write the answer on the lines provided.

1. This story is about:
   - ● why dogs shake water on us
   - ○ giving a dog a bath
   - ○ why dogs are funny

2. What might be one reason that dogs shake water on us?
   - ● They want to share the fun.
   - ○ We are standing too close to them.
   - ○ They don't have a towel.

3. Why do you think that dogs shake water on us?

   answers will vary

(6) | Total Problems: | Total Correct: | Score: | © Carson-Dellosa CD-2200

Name _____   Pretest

Read the story below.

Brandon had been fishing all morning. He had not caught any fish, and he was hungry. "I am going to get something to eat," he said. Brandon walked away. His little sister Michelle came over and picked up Brandon's fishing pole. Suddenly, it bent. A fish! Michelle pulled in a big fish. When Brandon came back, he was sorry he had left his pole.

Answer the questions. Fill in the circle beside the correct answer.

1. Why did Brandon leave his fishing pole?
   - ○ He was sleepy.
   - ● He was hungry.
   - ○ It was broken.

2. How long had Brandon been fishing?
   - ○ all afternoon
   - ○ all day
   - ● all morning

3. When Michelle picked up Brandon's fishing pole, it:
   - ● bent
   - ○ fell in the water
   - ○ broke

© Carson-Dellosa CD-2200 | Total Problems: | Total Correct: | Score: | (7)

Name _____

Read the story below.

This is Spot. Spot is a black and white dog. He likes to play fetch with Tom. Tom throws a stick. Spot runs to get the stick. Spot gives the stick to Tom. Then, they play again.

Answer the questions. Fill in the circle beside the correct answer.

1. Spot is a _____.
   ○ bird
   ○ cat
   ○ dog

2. What does Spot like to do with Tom?
   ○ run
   ○ fetch
   ○ dig

3. Spot is _____ and white.
   ○ brown
   ○ black
   ○ blue

Total Problems:	Total Correct:	Score:

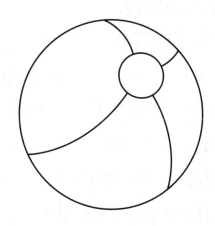

Read the story below.

Mark saw a new toy at the store. It was a blue and red ball. Mark told his mom about the ball. His mom said, "We will get it tomorrow." After Mark got the ball, he played with it every day.

Answer the questions. Fill in the circle beside the correct answer, or write the answer on the lines provided.

1. This story is about _____.
   ○ a new toy
   ○ the toy store
   ○ Mark's sister

2. The ball was blue and _____.
   ○ green
   ○ black
   ○ red

3. What does Mark's mom say about the ball?

   _____

   _____

10

| Total Problems: | Total Correct: | Score: |

Name _____

Read the story below.

   Sam likes to play ball after school. His friends come over to his house to play. They have fun throwing and catching the ball. When it gets dark outside, his friends go home. Sam goes in the house, too.

Answer the questions. Fill in the circle beside the correct answer, or write the answer on the lines provided.

1. Write the beginning letter of each picture on the line below it.

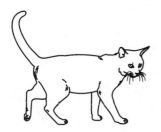      

_____   _____   _____

2. Sam likes to play _____.
   ○ video games
   ○ ball
   ○ cards

3. Sam likes to play ball with _____.
   ○ his friends
   ○ his mom
   ○ his dad

Total Problems:	Total Correct:	Score:

Read the story below.

   Maria's family is going on a trip. They have four bags to carry. The family is going to the beach. They are going to ride in a big jet. They will have fun on their trip.

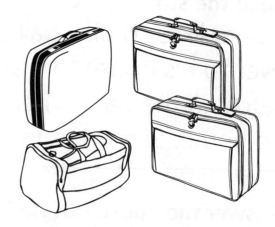

Answer the questions. Fill in the circle beside the correct answer, or write the answer on the lines provided.

1. Write the beginning letter of each picture on the line below it.

    _____et   _____ag   _____each

2. Maria's family is _____.
   ○ going on a trip
   ○ riding on a bike
   ○ packing bags

3. Her family is going to the _____.
   ○ park
   ○ museum
   ○ beach

12

| Total Problems: | Total Correct: | Score: |

Name _____

Find the words from the word box in the word search puzzle below. Circle the words you find.

Maria's Family Word Search

```
J  T  B  F  N  W  Q  S  B  G
E  L  R  I  A  H  O  Z  A  D
T  Q  M  I  G  M  H  B  M  Y
Z  P  R  N  P  C  I  H  S  T
B  F  L  Q  A  Y  R  L  C  Z
M  Y  Y  E  R  D  W  I  Y  E
W  A  B  R  N  B  S  Q  D  I
P  V  A  A  A  C  U  B  F  E
A  C  S  F  S  Z  B  K  S  N
F  U  N  R  O  M  A  G  V  B
```

Word Box				
bag	big	family	jet	sand
beach	carry	fun	ride	trip

Total Problems:	Total Correct:	Score:

Name _____

Read the story below.
   Pat has a red hat. She has a fat cat named Matt. Matt is sitting on a mat. Pat's cat saw a rat. Matt ran after the rat. The rat scared Pat.

Answer the questions. Fill in the circle beside the correct answer where appropriate.

1. Draw lines to connect the words below that rhyme.

sun	my
bee	duck
try	frog
truck	bun
dog	tree

2. Name each picture and listen for the vowel sound. Fill in the circle beside each correct vowel.

   ○ a   ○ e   ○ e   ○ i   ○ i   ○ u

3. Pat's cat is _____ .
   ○ fat   ○ mat   ○ rat

14

Total Problems:	Total Correct:	Score:

Circle the word that describes each picture below. Then, color the pictures.

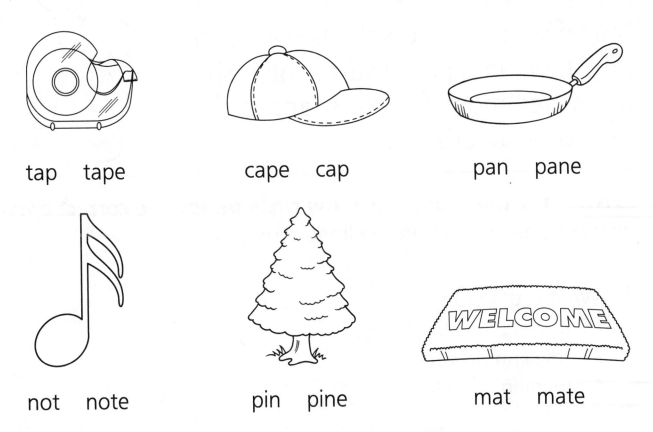

tap   tape   cape   cap   pan   pane

not   note   pin   pine   mat   mate

Color the picture red if you hear a long vowel sound. Color the picture green if you hear a short vowel sound.

| Total Problems: | Total Correct: | Score: |

Name _____

Read the story below.

Mary sees some pretty flowers in the garden. She thinks her mom would like the flowers. She picks the flowers and puts them in a pretty vase. Then, she gives her mom the vase and says, "Happy Mother's Day."

Answer the questions. Fill in the circle beside the correct answer, or write the answer on the lines provided.

1. What is this story about?
   - ○ flowers for Mary's mom
   - ○ smelling flowers
   - ○ reading a book

2. Write a **1**, **2**, or **3** on the line below each picture to show the correct order of the pictures.

_____ _____ _____

| Total Problems: | Total Correct: | Score: |

Circle the sentence that tells about each picture. Color the pictures.

1. The dog sat on the mat.
   The mat is on the dog.
   The dog is under the mat.

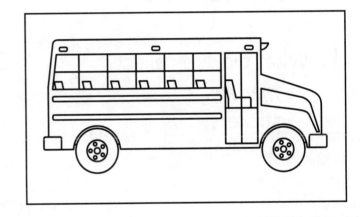

2. The bus is in the garage.
   The bus is empty.
   The bus is full of people.

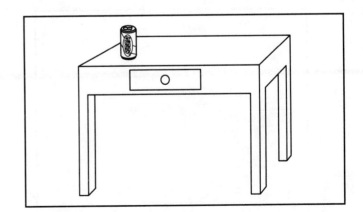

3. The cane is on the desk.
   The desk is on the cane.
   The can is on the desk.

Read the story below.

Joe loved to collect baseball cards. He loved to show his cards to all of his friends. Instead of stickers or candy, Joe wanted baseball cards. One day, he left his baseball collection on the school bus. When Joe got home, he was very sad. The bus driver gave Joe a box the next day. When Joe opened the box, his frown turned into a smile.

Answer the questions. Fill in the circle beside the correct answer where appropriate.

1. What did Joe collect?
   ○ marbles
   ○ stickers
   ○ baseball cards

2. Draw a picture of where Joe left his baseball cards.

3. What does the word "collect" mean?
   ○ to trade
   ○ to gather
   ○ to play

4. What do you think was inside the box that the bus driver gave to Joe?
   ○ stickers
   ○ candy
   ○ baseball cards

18

Total Problems:	Total Correct:	Score:

Read the story below.

Janet loves to draw pictures of butterflies. She draws pictures for her teacher, her friends, and her parents. Her butterflies have lots of colors. Janet made a book of butterflies for her mother. Her mother loved it!

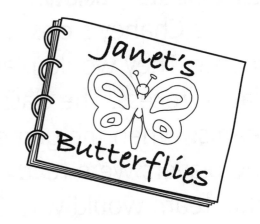

Answer the questions.

1. Write a **T** on the line if the statement is true. Write an **F** if the statement is false.

   _____ Janet likes to draw flowers.

   _____ Janet uses lots of colors.

   _____ Her mother loved the book of butterflies.

2. Circle the words that name colors below. Put an X on the words that are not colors.

   | yellow | ball | yarn |
   | friend | orange | blue |

Total Problems: _____   Total Correct: _____   Score: _____

Name _____

Read the story below.

   Miss Chaney's class loved to play soccer. They would play soccer every day at recess. The class would make two teams. When the game started, all of the players were ready. Sometimes the blue team would win. Sometimes the red team would win. Everyone played a good game as long as they tried their best.

_____

Answer the questions. Fill in the circle beside the correct answer.

1. Miss Chaney's class loved to play _____.
   ○ baseball
   ○ soccer
   ○ basketball

2. How many teams would the class make?
   ○ three
   ○ one
   ○ two

3. Did the red team win all of the time?
   ○ yes
   ○ no

4. When did Miss Chaney's class play soccer?
   ○ during recess
   ○ during math
   ○ during reading

Total Problems: _____   Total Correct: _____   Score: _____

Name _____

Circle the word that describes each picture below. Then, color the pictures.

kit   kite   cane   can   tub   tube

mope   mop   fin   fine

Color the picture red if you hear a long vowel sound. Color the picture green if you hear a short vowel sound.

Total Problems: ___   Total Correct: ___   Score: ___

Read the story below.

　Seeds come in different shapes, sizes, and colors. But, all seeds have one thing in common. All seeds have tiny plants inside them. When you plant a seed in the soil and give it water and sun, a sprout will grow. A sprout is a young plant that pops out of the seed. The sprout breaks through the soil to get some sun. The leaves on the sprout soak in the sunlight. The plant uses this sunlight to make food.

Answer the questions. Fill in the circle beside the correct answer, or write the answer on the lines provided.

1. Seeds come in different shapes, sizes, and _____.
   ○ textures
   ○ tastes
   ○ colors

2. How are all seeds alike?

   _____

3. What are the three things that seeds need to grow?
   ○ water, sun, salt
   ○ water, sun, soil
   ○ water, sun, shade

Total Problems:	Total Correct:	Score:

Name _____

Answer the questions.

4. Write a **T** on the line if the statement is true. Write an **F** if the statement is false.

_____ A sprout is an old plant.

_____ Sprouts can grow without water or sun.

_____ There is a tiny plant inside a seed.

_____ Plants make their food from sunlight.

5. Use the clues from the story to find the meanings of the words. Write the meanings on the lines below.

sprout: _____

_____

_____

soil: _____

_____

_____

6. Choose a word from the word box and write it under the picture it matches.

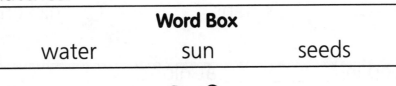

Word Box

water   sun   seeds

_____   _____   _____

| Total Problems: | Total Correct: | Score: |

Name _____

Read the story below.

   Many wild turkeys live in wooded areas of the United States. Many animals, like foxes and wolves, eat turkeys. To stay away from predators that might eat them, turkeys sleep in treetops at night. Turkeys love to eat acorns, grass, corn, and insects. They have good eyesight and hearing. Turkeys can fly for short periods of time, and they can run fast. Male turkeys are called toms, and females are called hens.

Answer the questions. Fill in the circle beside the correct answer, or write the answer on the lines provided.

1. Turkeys live in _____ areas of the United States.
   ○ wooded   ○ ocean   ○ grassy

2. Female turkeys are called _____.
   ○ toms   ○ hens   ○ chickens

3. Turkeys sleep in _____ at night.
   ○ water   ○ beds   ○ treetops

4. Name two animals that eat turkeys. _____

Total Problems: _____   Total Correct: _____   Score: _____

Answer the questions.

5. Draw a picture of the four things that turkeys eat. Label each picture on the line below it.

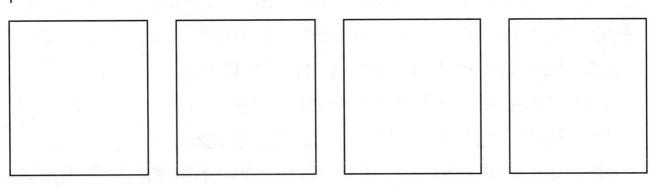

_____   _____   _____   _____

6. Write a **T** on the line if the statement is true. Write an **F** if the statement is false.

_____ Chickens like to eat turkeys.

_____ Turkeys do not run fast.

_____ Turkeys live in wooded areas.

_____ Turkeys can see well.

7. Use the clues from the story to find the meaning of the word. Write the meaning on the lines below.

predator: _____

_____

| Total Problems: | Total Correct: | Score: |

Read the story below.

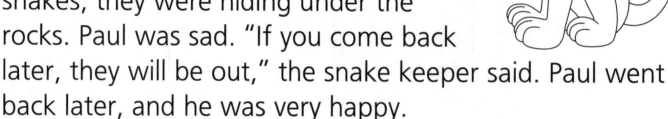

   Paul went to the zoo for his birthday. He wanted to see the bears, lions, and snakes. Paul saw the bears in their cage. He saw the lions running in the grass. But, when Paul went to see the snakes, they were hiding under the rocks. Paul was sad. "If you come back later, they will be out," the snake keeper said. Paul went back later, and he was very happy.

Answer the questions. Fill in the circle beside the correct answer.

1. Why did Paul go to the zoo?
   ○ for a field trip
   ○ for his birthday
   ○ for a family trip

2. How did Paul feel when the snakes were hiding?
   ○ He was excited.
   ○ He was sad.
   ○ He was angry.

3. Which animals did Paul see first?
   ○ lions   ○ snakes   ○ bears

Total Problems: _____   Total Correct: _____   Score: _____

Name _____

Find the words from the word box in the word search puzzle below. Circle the words you find.

Paul's Trip Word Search

```
C G R A S S B S H V
S A R M H Z A X O R
N H G O D R U O A W
A U U E C I Z E R I
K W Q I H K B E D O
E K P H C I P G K D
F F F A N E D T C Y
I O R O E C J I D B
J S I K K Z O U N J
X L S Z U N D E R G
```

Word Box				
bear	grass	keeper	rock	under
cage	hiding	lion	snake	zoo

Total Problems: Total Correct: Score:

Read the story below.

Garrett Morgan was born in Kentucky. He invented the gas mask, which was used to help people breathe through smoke and other gases. In 1923, Garrett Morgan invented the traffic signal. The traffic signal helped cars drive safely. The traffic light we use today comes from his invention.

Answer the questions. Fill in the circle beside the correct answer, or write the answer on the lines provided.

1. Garrett Morgan was born in _____.
   ○ Alabama
   ○ Georgia
   ○ Kentucky

2. How did the gas mask help people? _____

   _____

3. In what year was the traffic signal invented?
   ○ 1932
   ○ 1923
   ○ 1903

28 | Total Problems: _____ Total Correct: _____ Score: _____

Read the story below.

Jackie Robinson was born in Georgia. In 1947, Robinson became the first African-American to play baseball in the Major Leagues. He played for the Brooklyn Dodgers. Robinson was a great baseball player. After he left baseball, Robinson became a businessman. In 1962, he was invited to join the Baseball Hall of Fame.

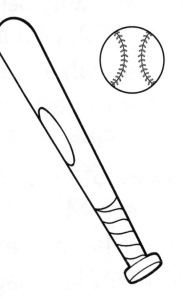

Answer the questions. Fill in the circle beside the correct answer.

1. Jackie Robinson was born in _____.
   ○ Tennessee
   ○ Georgia
   ○ New York

2. Jackie Robinson was the first African-American _____ in the Major Leagues.
   ○ football player
   ○ basketball player
   ○ baseball player

3. Jackie Robinson played for the Brooklyn _____.
   ○ Dodgers
   ○ Braves
   ○ Yankees

4. In _____, Jackie Robinson was invited to join the Baseball Hall of Fame.
   ○ 1947
   ○ 1960
   ○ 1962

Total Problems:	Total Correct:	Score:

Read the story below.

   In 1902, Marian Anderson was born in Philadelphia, Pennsylvania. She became the first African-American singer to perform at the Metropolitan Opera House. In 1939, Eleanor Roosevelt, the wife of the president of the United States, asked Anderson to perform an outdoor concert. More than 75,000 people came to hear her sing. Marian went to Europe and learned to sing in nine different languages. In 1945, the Marian Anderson Award was formed to help other singers.

Answer the questions. Fill in the circle beside the correct answer.

1. In what year was Marian Anderson born?
   ○ 1993
   ○ 1945
   ○ 1902

2. Eleanor Roosevelt asked her to sing at _____.
   ○ an indoor concert
   ○ an outdoor concert
   ○ a party

3. How many languages did she learn in Europe?
   ○ six
   ○ eight
   ○ nine

4. Marian Anderson was the first African-American singer to perform at:
   ○ the Metropolitan Opera House
   ○ Radio City Music Hall
   ○ the White House

Total Problems: _____   Total Correct: _____   Score: _____

Read the story below.

   Thurgood Marshall was born in 1908 in Maryland. He attended Howard University, where he studied to become a lawyer. In 1952, Thurgood Marshall won the case that would eliminate, or end, school segregation. This meant that all students of any color could go to the same school. In 1967, President Johnson named Marshall to the Supreme Court of the United States. He was the first African-American Supreme Court judge.

Answer the questions. Fill in the circle beside the correct answer.

1. Thurgood Marshall was born in 1908 in _____.
   - ○ Maryland
   - ○ Utah
   - ○ Maine

2. What did Thurgood Marshall become?
   - ○ a teacher
   - ○ an artist
   - ○ a lawyer

3. In the story, what does the word "eliminate" mean?
   - ○ ask
   - ○ end
   - ○ start

Read the story below.

Jay wants to go outside to ride his new bike. He puts on his new helmet and his tennis shoes. When he gets downstairs, his mom says, "You can't go outside." "Why not?" asks Jay. "It is raining," his mom replies. Jay takes off his helmet and tennis shoes. Jay looks out the window and sighs. When the rain stops, Jay rides his bike.

Answer the questions. Fill in the circle beside the correct answer, or write the answer on the lines provided.

1. Jay wants to go outside to
   _____.
   ○ play ball
   ○ walk the dog
   ○ ride his bike

2. What does Jay put on his head to protect himself?
   ○ his hat
   ○ his helmet
   ○ his tennis shoes

3. Why does Jay sigh?
   ○ He likes the rain.
   ○ His bike is broken.
   ○ He is sad because he can't go outside.

4. What do you think Jay did until it stopped raining?

   _____

   _____

Total Problems: _____   Total Correct: _____   Score: _____

Name _____

Find the words from the word box in the word search puzzle below. Circle the words you find.

It's Raining Word Search

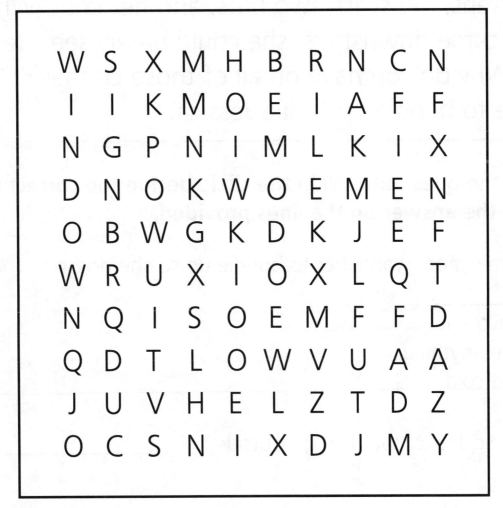

```
W S X M H B R N C N
I I K M O E I A F F
N G P N I M L K I X
D N O K W O E M E N
O B W G K D K J E F
W R U X I O X L Q T
N Q I S O E M F F D
Q D T L O W V U A A
J U V H E L Z T D Z
O C S N I X D J M Y
```

Word Box

bike	look	new	rain	shoe
helmet	mom	outside	sign	window

Total Problems: _____ Total Correct: _____ Score: _____

33

Read the story below.

Jessica wanted to go outside and play in the snow. Her mom said, "Bundle up! It's cold outside." So Jessica put on two sweaters. Then, she put on three pairs of pants, her mittens, her scarf, two hats, and her coat. When Jessica came downstairs, she could barely see. Her mom said, "Why do you have on all of those clothes?" "You told me to bundle up!" said Jessica.

Answer the questions. Fill in the circle beside the correct answer, or write the answer on the lines provided.

1. Jessica's mom wants her to bundle up so she doesn't

    _____.
    ○ have fun
    ○ see anything
    ○ get cold

2. Why did Jessica want to go outside? _____

    _____

3. How many sweaters did Jessica put on?
    ○ five
    ○ two
    ○ three

Total Problems: _____   Total Correct: _____   Score: _____

Answer the questions.

4. Write a **1**, **2**, **3**, **4**, or **5** on each line below to show the order she put her clothes on.

_____ pants

_____ hats

_____ coat

_____ scarf

_____ sweaters

5. Color the hat that tells what the story was mostly about.

Jessica wanted to build a snowman.

Jessica had to dress warmly before she went outside.

6. Choose a word from the word box and write it under the picture it matches.

Word Box		
hat	scarf	mitten

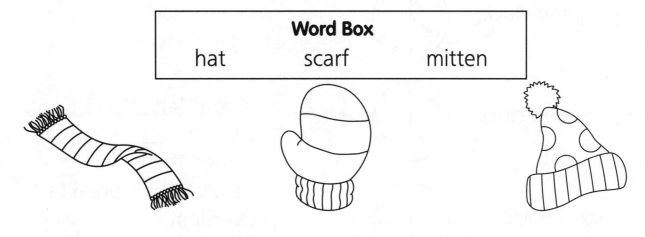

_____   _____   _____

Total Problems:	Total Correct:	Score:

Read the story below.

Scott got ready for bed. He took a bath, brushed his teeth, and combed his hair. Scott was ready for a good night's sleep. Scott set his alarm clock to wake him up at seven o'clock. Scott 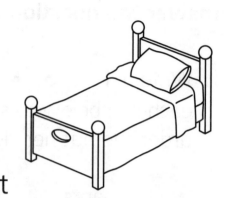 put his head on the pillow and fell asleep quickly. When Scott's clock rang, he turned it off and went back to sleep. Scott finally woke up at nine o'clock. Scott jumped out of bed and ran to get dressed. When Scott got to school, his teacher told him he was late.

Answer the questions. Fill in the circle beside the correct answer.

1. Which clock shows the time Scott wanted to get up?

   ○ eight o'clock

   ○ seven o'clock

   ○ six o'clock

2. What time did school probably start?
   ○ six o'clock
   ○ nine o'clock
   ○ eight o'clock

3. Scott was late to school because he _____.
   ○ missed the bus
   ○ slowly ate his breakfast
   ○ overslept

Total Problems: ___   Total Correct: ___   Score: ___

Name _____

Find the words from the word box in the word search puzzle below. Circle the words you find.

What Time Is It? Word Search

```
O  B  Q  X  G  V  Q  U  B  O
E  R  A  U  O  T  L  M  W  T
J  P  Z  T  R  X  O  O  X  B
V  J  I  S  H  C  L  K  N  C
B  V  J  P  C  L  D  Q  Y  L
R  D  Y  U  I  H  H  H  Z  O
U  X  C  P  V  O  O  A  E  C
S  S  D  M  F  V  O  O  I  K
H  E  V  N  V  X  H  O  L  R
B  A  L  A  R  M  H  J  J  Z
```

Word Box

alarm	brush	comb	pillow
bath	clock	hair	school

Read the story below.

Lisa had a rabbit named Fluffy. She kept Fluffy in a cage in her bedroom. Lisa would feed, pet, and play with Fluffy every day after school. When Lisa got home from school one day, Fluffy was not in her cage. "Where is Fluffy?" Lisa wondered. She looked in Fluffy's favorite hiding places. First, she looked under the bed. Then, she looked in the closet. She looked in the toy chest last. Lisa couldn't find Fluffy anywhere. "Where is Fluffy?" Lisa asked aloud. Lisa's mom came into her room with Fluffy in her arms. "Fluffy is with me. I just cleaned her cage," her mom said. Lisa was happy that Fluffy was safe.

Answer the questions. Fill in the circle beside the correct answer.

1. Fluffy is Lisa's pet _____.
   ○ rabbit
   ○ hamster
   ○ frog

2. Lisa feeds, pets, and _____ with Fluffy.
   ○ hops
   ○ plays
   ○ eats

3. Lisa was _____ when she couldn't find Fluffy.
   ○ worried
   ○ angry
   ○ confused

4. What did Lisa ask when she didn't see Fluffy in the cage?
   ○ "Where is my rabbit?"
   ○ "Who has Fluffy?"
   ○ "Where is Fluffy?"

| Total Problems: | Total Correct: | Score: |

Name _____

Answer the questions.

5. Write a 1, 2, or 3 on the line below each picture to show the order that Lisa looked for Fluffy.

 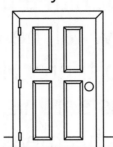 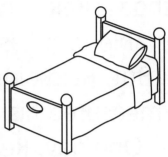

_____   _____   _____

6. Write a **T** on the line if the statement is true. Write an **F** if the statement is false.

_____ Lisa looked for Fluffy in the garage.

_____ Lisa did not look in Fluffy's cage.

_____ Lisa was happy to see Fluffy with her mom.

7. What do you think Fluffy looks like? Draw Fluffy below.

Total Problems:	Total Correct:	Score:

Read the story below.

Reid always asked his mom questions. One of his favorite questions was, "How tall am I?" So, for his birthday, Reid's mom got him a measuring tape. Reid was able to measure how tall he was. He was 48 inches tall. But, Reid didn't stop there. He measured everything. He measured his arm, his ear, his leg, his foot, and his hair. One day, Reid took his measuring tape to school. He wanted to see how tall his friends were. During recess, he measured all of his friends. Reid loved his birthday present!

Answer the questions. Fill in the circle beside the correct answer.

1. What did Reid always ask his mother?
   ○ "How big am I?"
   ○ "How short am I?"
   ○ "How tall am I?"

2. What did Reid's mother buy him for his birthday?
   ○ a ruler
   ○ a measuring tape
   ○ stickers

3. How tall was Reid?
   ○ 48 inches   ○ 40 inches   ○ 63 inches

Total Problems: _____   Total Correct: _____   Score: _____

Name _____

Find the words from the word box in the word search puzzle below. Circle the words you find.

How Tall Am I? Word Search

```
T  S  L  E  G  F  L  K  F  W
L  A  T  F  R  R  O  U  G  V
A  N  P  O  O  E  E  E  D  D
O  U  G  E  P  O  C  B  Y  E
Z  A  K  P  M  H  T  E  R  N
J  F  Q  C  S  C  M  U  S  L
J  G  Y  H  T  F  S  H  L  S
E  M  J  F  F  A  C  A  M  C
A  A  P  K  E  N  T  R  P  X
R  H  Z  M  I  B  A  W  J  M
```

Word Box				
arm	foot	leg	recess	tall
ear	inch	measure	stop	tape

Total Problems: Total Correct: Score:

41

Name _____

Read the story below.

On Monday, Miss Smith's class talked about safety. Each student gave a safety tip to the class. Alex said, "You should wear a helmet when you ride your bike." Sarah said, "You should wear a life jacket when you are in a boat." "If you play football, you should wear a helmet and shoulder pads," said Joe. After they finished talking about safety, the class cut out pictures of their safety tips.

Answer the questions. Fill in the circle beside the correct answer, or write the answer on the lines provided.

1. Who cut out each picture below?

○ Alex
○ Joe
○ Sarah

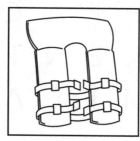

○ Alex
○ Joe
○ Sarah

○ Alex
○ Joe
○ Sarah

2. Write your own safety tip. _____

_____

Total Problems:	Total Correct:	Score:

Find the words from the word box in the word search puzzle below. Circle the words you find.

Safety Rules Word Search

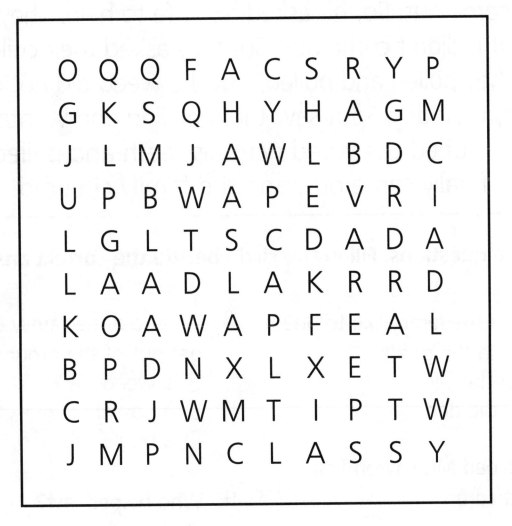

```
O Q Q F A C S R Y P
G K S Q H Y H A G M
J L M J A W L B D C
U P B W A P E V R I
L G L T S C D A D A
L A A D L A K R R D
K O A W A P F E A L
B P D N X L X E T W
C R J W M T I P T W
J M P N C L A S S Y
```

Word Box				
always	class	jacket	play	tip
boat	draw	pad	safety	wear

Read the story below.

   The Layton family loved to plant in their garden.
Everyone pitched in to help. One day, Mr. Layton tried to
pull a weed out of the ground. He pulled and pulled, but
it didn't come out. So, he asked his wife to help. They
pulled, but it didn't come out. So, they asked their children
to help. They pulled and pulled, but the weed did not come
out. Then, their dog Spot saw them pulling and wanted to
help. He grabbed the weed with his teeth and pulled.
The weed finally came out, and the family cheered!

Answer the questions. Fill in the circle beside the correct answer.

1. What did the family like to do?
   - ○ plant in the garden
   - ○ wash the car
   - ○ walk the dog

2. Who helped Mr. Layton first?
   - ○ his children
   - ○ the dog
   - ○ his wife

3. What did the family try to get out of the ground?
   - ○ a weed
   - ○ a flower
   - ○ a bug

4. Who helped last?
   - ○ the father
   - ○ the dog
   - ○ the children

| Total Problems: | Total Correct: | Score: |

Name _____

Answer the questions.

5. Write a **1**, **2**, or **3** in the box below each picture to show the correct order in which the family helped.

6. Color the pictures of the tools the family will need to take care of their garden.

| Total Problems: | Total Correct: | Score: |

Read the story below.

Tim loves golf. His parents bought him golf clubs and a box of golf balls. Instead of cartoons, Tim watches golf on television. He practices golf in his backyard every day after school. He takes his golf clubs and balls outside. He sets the ball on the golf tee. Then, he swings the golf club and hits the ball. One day, the ball went sailing through the air into his neighbor's yard. Tim heard a loud noise and became worried. Then, Tim's mom came outside and asked what the sound was.

Answer the questions. Fill in the circle beside the correct answer.

1. Tim likes to play _____.
   ○ basketball
   ○ soccer
   ○ golf

2. Tim's parents bought him _____.
   ○ golf clubs and balls
   ○ a baseball
   ○ a football

3. What do you think happened?
   ○ Tim's golf club broke.
   ○ Tim's golf ball cracked.
   ○ Tim broke his neighbor's window.

4. How does Tim feel?
   ○ happy
   ○ mad
   ○ worried

Total Problems: _____ Total Correct: _____ Score: _____

Name _____

Read the story below.

   Anita has to clean her room once a week. Her room was very messy today! Anita started to hang her clothes in the closet and put her toys in the toy chest. Then, Anita noticed it was one o'clock. It was time for her favorite television show. Anita had not finished cleaning, so she pushed the rest of the toys under the bed. Anita ran downstairs and turned on the television. "Did you finish cleaning your room, Anita?" her mom asked. "Not exactly," Anita said. Anita knew she had to turn off the television and go upstairs.

Answer the questions. Fill in the circle beside the correct answer.

1. Anita cleans her room _____.
   ○ every day
   ○ every Monday
   ○ once a week

2. Anita started to hang her clothes in the _____.
   ○ chest
   ○ closet
   ○ bathroom

Answer the questions.

1. In the word box, color the squares with the color words orange. Color the verbs blue. Color the number words yellow. Color the nouns green.

Word Box

white	jump	two
dog	black	teacher
hop	car	blue
one	run	green

2. Choose a word from the word box that best completes each sentence. Write the words on the lines provided.

The _____ drove down the street.

The rabbit likes to _____.

The _____ gave the class homework.

I have _____ ears.

The sky is _____.

Total Problems: _____ Total Correct: _____ Score: _____

Circle the sentence that tells about each picture. Color the pictures.

1. The cloud is over the city.
   The plow is in the field.
   The clown is in the park.

2. The girl plays with a top.
   The girl plays with a doll.
   The girl plays on a team.

3. Judy walks to school.
   Judy runs to the bus stop.
   Judy rides to the store.

Total Problems:	Total Correct:	Score:

Read the story below.

Lindsey and Jessica were best friends. They did everything together. One day, Jessica's parents told her that they were going to move. Jessica was very upset. When she told Lindsey, Lindsey was sad. "Who will be my best friend now?" Lindsey asked. Jessica said, "I will. We can still write and visit each other." When Jessica moved away, the girls kept in touch like they had promised.

Answer the questions. Fill in the circle beside the correct answer, or write the answer on the lines provided.

1. The girls were _____.
   ○ enemies
   ○ sisters
   ○ best friends

2. How did Jessica feel when her parents told her they were going to move?
   ○ happy
   ○ upset
   ○ excited

3. What would be a good title for this story?
   ○ Getting a New Friend
   ○ Moving
   ○ My Friend Moved Away

4. How would you feel if you were Lindsey?

   _____

   _____

   _____

Total Problems: _____   Total Correct: _____   Score: _____

Find the words from the word box in the word search puzzle below. Circle the words you find.

A Friend Like Jessica Word Search

```
M E S Y D Y E S N T
K O C A I I U D S O
M L V L D B N E B C
S J O E O E B W S K
C H R C I T X T W O
H U K R T W H U E G
O I F I I W R E T T
O W S Q Y M F I S V
L I P F I D U P T G
V P A R E N T W I E
```

Word Box				
best	clothes	move	sad	visit
bus	friend	parent	school	write

Total Problems: Total Correct: Score:

Name _____

Read the story below.

Linda and Mom love to bake. They bake cakes and brownies. But, their favorite thing to bake is cookies. First, Linda takes out the flour, milk, eggs, and chocolate chips. She mixes the dough in a bowl. She makes little balls with the dough and places them on the cookie sheet. Then, Linda's mom puts the cookies into the oven while Linda finishes her homework. "What is that smell?" Mom suddenly asks. "Oh, my cookies!" yells Linda. Linda runs into the kitchen and opens the oven.

Answer the questions. Fill in the circle beside the correct answer.

1. What do Linda and her mom love to bake?
   ○ pies
   ○ cookies
   ○ bread

2. Which ingredient did Linda not use to make her cookies?
   ○ eggs
   ○ flour
   ○ apples

3. What do you think happened to their cookies?
   ○ They burned.
   ○ They were too small.
   ○ They tasted good.

4. What would be a good title for this story?
   ○ The Good Cookies
   ○ The Burned Cookies
   ○ The Good Cake

52

| Total Problems: | Total Correct: | Score: |

Name _____

Answer the questions.

5. Describe how you think Linda's cookies could have been saved.

_____

_____

_____

_____

6. What caused Linda's cookies to burn in the oven?
   - ○ She was doing her homework.
   - ○ She didn't turn on the oven.
   - ○ She fell asleep.

7. Draw a picture of what you think Linda's cookies looked like when she opened the oven.

Read the story below.

   Ms. Proctor's class had a jack-o'-lantern contest. The student who could carve the best pumpkin would win a trip to the candy store. Everyone brought in pumpkins. Joe and Scott both wanted to win the contest. First, they drew the faces on their pumpkins. Then, they each cut out eyes, a nose, and a mouth. Each boy knew he had to do his best if he was going to win. The next day, the principal came into the class to judge. He thought Joe's and Scott's pumpkins were great. But, the principal could only pick one. The principal said, "The winner is. . ."

_____

Answer the questions. Write the answers on the lines provided.

1. Ms. Proctor's class decided to have a _____.

2. What would the winner of the contest get?

_____

3. The _____ judged the contest.

4. Scott and Joe knew they had to do their _____ if they wanted to win.

Total Problems: _____   Total Correct: _____   Score: _____

Answer the questions.

5. Follow the directions below to make Joe's and Scott's jack-o'-lanterns.

Scott

Joe

Draw two triangles for the eyes.

Draw one square for the nose.

Draw a smiling mouth with

two teeth.

Color the pumpkin orange.

Color the stem green.

Draw two circles for the eyes.

Draw one rectangle for the nose.

Draw a frowning mouth with five teeth.

Color the pumpkin orange.

Color the stem green.

_____

6. Who do you think won the contest? Color the ribbon blue for the person you think should win the contest.

Scott

Joe

Total Problems:	Total Correct:	Score:

Name _____

Read the story below.

    Tonight is pizza night at the Marion house. Delaney and Troy get a pepperoni pizza. Their parents get a cheese pizza. When the pizzas are delivered, they sit down to eat. Each pizza has twelve slices. So, everyone gets six slices each. Mom and Dad eat all of their pizza. But, Delaney has two slices left. "May I have your two slices of pizza?" asks Troy. "Yes," says Delaney.

Answer the questions. Fill in the circle beside the correct answer, or write the answer on the lines provided.

1. How many pizzas did the family order?
   - ○ three
   - ○ two
   - ○ four

2. What type of pizza did Delaney eat?
   - ○ pepperoni
   - ○ cheese
   - ○ mushroom

3. Each pizza had _____ slices.

4. How many slices of pizza did Mom eat?
   - ○ ten
   - ○ twelve
   - ○ six

5. If Troy ate his slices of pizza, then ate Delaney's slices, how many slices of pizza did he eat in all?
   - ○ ten
   - ○ eight
   - ○ six

Total Problems: Total Correct: Score:

Name _____

Find the words from the word box in the word search puzzle below. Circle the words you find.

Pizza Night Word Search

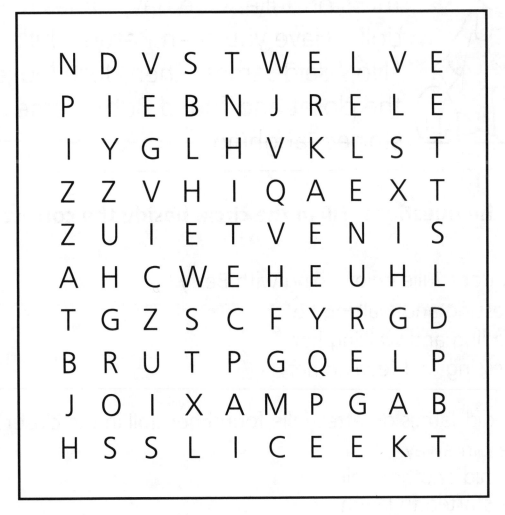

```
N  D  V  S  T  W  E  L  V  E
P  I  E  B  N  J  R  E  L  E
I  Y  G  L  H  V  K  L  S  T
Z  Z  V  H  I  Q  A  E  X  T
Z  U  I  E  T  V  E  N  I  S
A  H  C  W  E  H  E  U  H  L
T  G  Z  S  C  F  Y  R  G  D
B  R  U  T  P  G  Q  E  L  P
J  O  I  X  A  M  P  G  A  B
H  S  S  L  I  C  E  E  K  T
```

Word Box				
all	deliver	house	pizza	slice
cheese	eat	night	sit	twelve

Total Problems: _____   Total Correct: _____   Score: _____

Read the story below.

Julie loves to dress and feed her doll, Betty. She even has tea parties with Betty. Julie's brother James likes to play tricks on Julie. One day, James hid Julie's doll. "Have you seen Betty?" Julie asked. "No," said James. Then, Julie looked in the closet and found Betty. James started laughing.

Answer the questions. Fill in the circle beside the correct answer.

1. What does Julie enjoy doing with Betty?
   ○ dressing and walking her
   ○ feeding and walking her
   ○ dressing and feeding her

2. What did James do after Julie found her doll in the closet?
   ○ He ran away.
   ○ He hid another doll.
   ○ He started to laugh.

3. Do you think James will hide Julie's doll again? Why or why not?

   _____

   _____

58   Total Problems: _____   Total Correct: _____   Score: _____

Circle the sentence that tells about each picture. Color the pictures.

1. His mitten did not fit.
   William sits on the rug.
   I can fix the fan.

3. Dan will hit the ball.
   Dan will hit the bat.
   Jan washes the car.

2. I will run to get the cab.
   Hank is wearing a new cap.
   Jill was in the cab.

4. Katrina counts the coins.
   Katrina runs the bases.
   Katrina walks to school.

Total Problems:	Total Correct:	Score:

Name _____

Read the story below.

   Your body is made up of many systems. Your bones are part of your skeletal system. Your body is made up of 206 bones. Bones give your body its shape. If you did not have a skeleton, you would look like a rag doll. Your bones are hard and help you stand and sit. Vitamin D keeps your bones and teeth strong and healthy. Vitamin D is found in foods like milk and fish.

_____

Answer the questions. Fill in the circle beside the correct answer, or write the answer on the lines provided.

1. Your body is made up of

   _____ bones.

2. Bones give your body its

   _____.

3. Your bones make up your

   _____.
   - ○ bone system
   - ○ skeletal system
   - ○ strong system

4. Your bones are _____.
   - ○ soft
   - ○ rubber
   - ○ hard

5. Which vitamin helps to keep your bones and teeth healthy?
   - ○ vitamin A
   - ○ vitamin C
   - ○ vitamin D

Total Problems: _____   Total Correct: _____   Score: _____

Find the words from the word box in the word search puzzle below. Circle the words you find.

The Skeletal System Word Search

```
S  L  T  V  I  T  A  M  I  N
Y  K  H  I  S  H  A  P  E  Y
C  R  E  A  I  M  U  K  D  O
C  Z  Y  L  R  B  Z  O  Y  T
S  B  U  R  E  D  B  H  J  S
T  O  I  D  J  T  T  M  E  Y
R  N  Y  M  K  L  O  D  E  S
O  E  P  L  A  F  I  N  G  T
N  S  I  E  G  S  M  P  K  E
G  M  H  G  G  D  A  L  D  M
```

Word Box				
body	hard	milk	skeleton	system
bones	healthy	shape	strong	vitamin

Read the story below.

Your muscular system is very important. Muscles make your body move. There are more than 650 muscles in your body. There are three types of muscles. Some muscles help you move. They are called skeletal muscles. Some muscles help your other organs work, and they are called smooth muscles. Your heart is a muscle. It is called the cardiac muscle. Your muscles need energy to work. You get energy from foods that have vitamins B and D, like vegetables, fish, peanuts, and wheat.

Answer the questions. Fill in the circle beside the correct answer, or write the answer on the lines provided.

1. How many muscles make up the muscular system?
   ○ over 206   ○ over 700   ○ over 650

2. Name the three types of muscles in your body.

   _____

   _____

3. Your muscles need _____ to work.
   ○ energy   ○ bones   ○ water

Total Problems:	Total Correct:	Score:

Name _____

Find the words from the word box in the word search puzzle below. Circle the words you find

The Muscular System Word Search

```
V  N  Z  M  U  S  C  L  E  S
X  E  W  C  H  E  A  R  T  E
N  O  G  O  T  J  F  R  V  D
A  R  U  E  R  V  F  O  C  S
E  G  O  T  T  K  M  A  C  M
N  A  P  R  N  A  I  X  J  O
E  N  S  Z  D  D  B  C  S  O
R  S  N  E  R  M  W  L  L  T
G  S  F  A  G  J  Y  D  E  H
Y  I  C  Y  T  H  R  E  E  S
```

Word Box

cardiac	heart	muscles	smooth	vegetables
energy	move	organs	three	work

© Carson-Dellosa CD-2200

Total Problems:	Total Correct:	Score:

Name _____

Read the story below.

   Your digestive system starts to work as soon as you put food in your mouth. Your mouth chews and breaks down the food. Saliva mixes with the food to make it easier to swallow. When you swallow, the food travels from your esophagus to your stomach. Your stomach turns the food into a thick soup. Then, it travels to your small intestine. Your small intestine takes out vitamins and minerals and sends them to your blood. The rest of the food travels to your large intestine, where most of the water is taken out. The rest leaves your body as waste. It takes three days for food to go through your entire digestive system.

Answer the questions. Write the answers on the lines provided.

1. The digestive system starts in your _____.

2. What mixes with food to make it easier for you to swallow?

_____

3. What does your stomach do?

_____

_____

4. The small intestine takes out

_____ and

_____.

Total Problems: _____ Total Correct: _____ Score: _____

Name _____

Find the words from the word box in the word search puzzle below. Circle the words you find.

The Digestive System Word Search

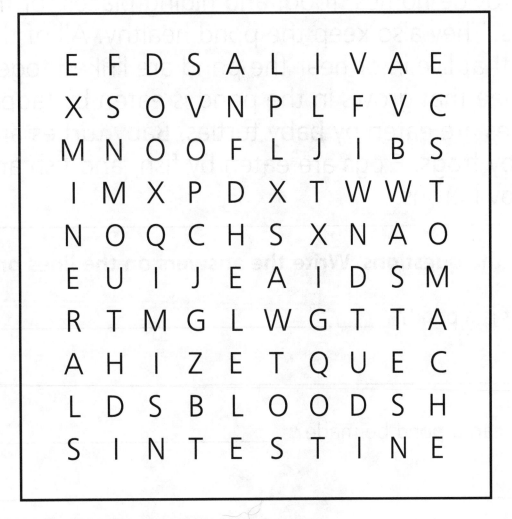

```
E F D S A L I V A E
X S O V N P L F V C
M N O O F L J I B S
I M X P D X T W W T
N O Q C H S X N A O
E U I J E A I D S M
R T M G L W G T T A
A H I Z E T Q U E C
L D S B L O O D S H
S I N T E S T I N E
```

Word Box

blood	esophagus	intestine	mouth	stomach
digestive	food	minerals	saliva	waste

Read the story below.

 A pond is an area of fresh, still water. It can be made by nature or by man. Many different plants, insects, and animals live in a pond. Pond plants are very important. They provide homes, food, and hiding places for many animals. They also keep the pond healthy. All of the things that live in or near the pond are linked together. The algae that grows in the pond is eaten by tadpoles. Tadpoles are eaten by baby turtles. Baby turtles are eaten by frogs. Frogs are eaten by fish, and fish are eaten by herons.

Answer the questions. Write the answers on the lines provided.

1. What is a pond? _____

   _____

2. How can a pond be made? _____

   _____

3. How do insects and animals depend on pond plants?

   _____

   _____

Total Problems: _____   Total Correct: _____   Score: _____

Answer the questions.

4. Write a 1, 2, 3, 4, 5, or 6 on the line below each picture in the order that the plants and animals are linked together.

_____

_____

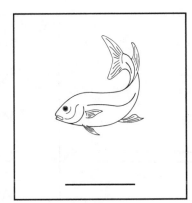

_____

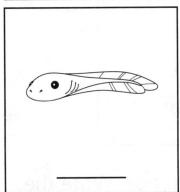

_____

_____

_____

5. Follow the directions below to draw a picture of a pond.

First, draw three fish in the pond.

Add two turtles swimming.

Next, draw four lily pads on top of the water.

Add a frog sitting on each lily pad.

Last, color the picture.

Answer the questions.

1. Draw a line from each contraction in the left column to the words in the right column that form it.

didn't	can not
isn't	have not
wasn't	are not
can't	is not
weren't	could not
aren't	did not
haven't	was not
couldn't	were not

2. Study the underlined contraction in each sentence. Write the words that form the contraction on the lines provided.

I'll go to the store. _____

She hasn't finished her lunch. _____

Jenny won't leave yet. _____

You shouldn't run. _____

We're hungry. _____

| Total Problems: ____ Total Correct: ____ Score: ____ |

Name _____

Circle the word that best completes each sentence. Write the word on the line provided.

1. _____ going to the store.	She'll She's
2. _____ eaten all of the pizza.	I've I'm
3. _____ my favorite picture.	Let's That's
4. _____ my best friend.	He'll He's
5. _____ be back soon.	They'll They've
6. Brandon _____ washing the car.	isn't didn't
7. Mom _____ be late for dinner.	aren't shouldn't
8. Dad _____ win the race.	wasn't didn't

Total Problems: **Total Correct:**   **Score:**

Read the story below.

Tim's friend Roger has a puppy named Spot. One day, Tim asked his parents for a puppy. His father said, "A puppy is a big job. You have to feed him, brush him, take him for walks, and bathe him." Tim said, "If you get me a puppy, I'll do all of the work." Tim's family went to the pet store the next day. Tim looked in the window and picked out a puppy. "What are you going to name him?" his mom asked. "Spot," said Tim.

Answer the questions. Write the answers on the lines provided.

1. Why do you think Tim wanted a puppy?

_____

2. Why do you think Roger named his dog Spot?

_____

3. When Tim asked his parents for a dog, what did his dad say?

_____

4. Why do you think Tim named his dog Spot?

_____

Total Problems:	Total Correct:	Score:

Find the words from the word box in the word search puzzle below. Circle the words you find.

Tim's New Puppy Word Search

```
L R W H I T E K P P
A H L Y E M L M S U
C R Z F F A U X T P
Q A F O W J M Q O P
Y B R S K Q O D R Y
C O R C P Q V R E M
E K A U F O B Y C G
W L V B S E T O K Q
B O W K L H E R I K
G H H R L Q M D P C
```

Word Box				
black	car	jump	spot	walk
brush	feed	puppy	store	white

Read the story below.

   A mother butterfly lays a tiny, white egg on a leaf. The egg pops open two weeks later, and a small caterpillar comes out. The caterpillar eats and eats until it gets fat. Most caterpillars like to eat plant leaves and grasses. Then, the caterpillar finds a safe place and builds a silky covering around its body called a chrysalis. The caterpillar stays in the chrysalis for about two weeks. When the chrysalis opens, a beautiful butterfly emerges. The butterfly allows its wings to dry and then flies away.

Answer the questions. Write the answers on the lines provided.

1. Where does the mother butterfly place her egg?

   _____

2. What pops out of the egg?

   _____

3. What does the caterpillar do when it pops out of the egg?

   _____

4. Name two things that a caterpillar eats.

   _____

Total Problems: _____   Total Correct: _____   Score: _____

Name _____

Find the words from the word box in the word search puzzle below. Circle the words you find.

From a Caterpillar to a Butterfly Word Search

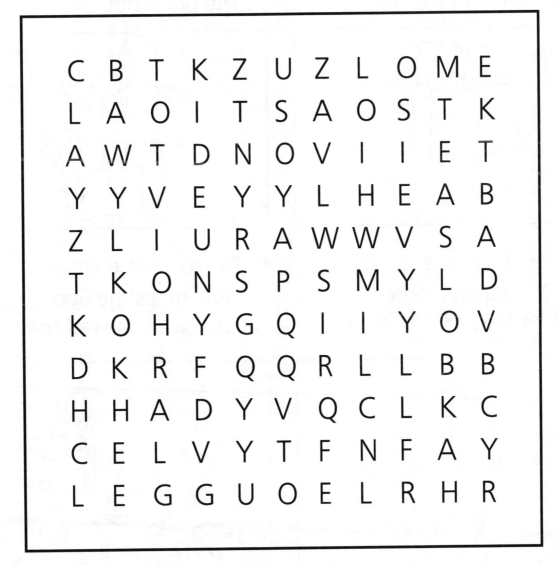

```
C B T K Z U Z L O M E
L A O I T S A O S T K
A W T D N O V I I E T
Y Y V E Y Y L H E A B
Z L I U R A W W V S A
T K O N S P S M Y L D
K O H Y G Q I I Y O V
D K R F Q Q R L L B B
H H A D Y V Q C L K C
C E L V Y T F N F A Y
L E G G U O E L R H R
```

Word Box				
body	chrysalis	lay	silky	week
caterpillar	egg	leaf	tiny	white

Total Problems: _____   Total Correct: _____   Score: _____

Name _____

Circle the sentence that tells about each picture. Color the pictures.

1. The tag is on the bag.
   The cat is on the mat.
   The man is in the van.

3. Dan has a big dog.
   Erin is sad.
   The pot is hot.

2. Her dad has a cane.
   Liz is wearing a cape.
   Pat hit the ball with a bat.

4. The fox is in the log.
   Irene mops the floor.
   Joey sat in the red chair.

Total Problems: **Total Correct:**   **Score:**

Read the letter below.

November 29, 2003

Dear Jane,

   I am glad that you came from Florida to visit me. I had a lot of fun playing with our dolls and other toys. I liked playing ball in my backyard. I had a great time when we made cookies together. I hope we can see each other again soon. Maybe I can visit you in Florida next time. I hope you had a good time, too.

Love,
Jill

Answer the questions. Fill in the circle beside the correct answer, or write the answer on the lines provided.

1. Who wrote the letter?
   ○ Jane   ○ Jill   ○ Florida

2. Name two things that the girls did together. _____

   _____

3. Where does Jane live? _____

4. When was the letter written?
   ○ November 12   ○ November 10   ○ November 29

| Total Problems: | Total Correct: | Score: |

Read the letter below.

June 16, 2001

Dear Joe,

Can you go fishing with me? I have asked five other classmates to come. We will be leaving from my house on Saturday morning at four o'clock. My dad says we have to be awake before the fish. We will bait our hooks and catch as many fish as we can. Please come!

Your friend,
Alex

Answer the questions. Fill in the circle beside the correct answer, or write the answer on the lines provided.

1. What are they going to do on the boat? _____

2. How many classmates can Alex invite in all? _____

3. In what month was the letter written?
   ○ July
   ○ January
   ○ June

4. What time are they leaving Alex's house? _____

Total Problems:	Total Correct:	Score:

Name _____

Read the letter below.

September 13, 2010

Dear Uncle Charles,

It is the beginning of school. I am in the first grade this year. My teacher says we will learn a lot of new things, like how to read, write, add, and subtract. The best thing about first grade is we will go on field trips! We are going to the museum in December. My teacher said we can bring someone with us. Could you go with me? I hope you can!

Love,
Anne

Answer the questions. Fill in the circle beside the correct answer, or write the answer on the lines provided.

1. Who is the letter for?
   ○ the teacher   ○ Anne   ○ Uncle Charles

2. What grade is Anne in? _____

3. Name two things Anne will learn in first grade. _____

_____

Total Problems:	Total Correct:	Score:

Read the letter below.

December 5, 2005

Dear Jamal,

   Did you lose your baseball cards? My mom was cleaning out the car, and she found a stack of baseball cards. You probably left them after our scout meeting yesterday. I put them in a box. Please come to my house and look through them. I think they are yours.

Thanks,
Scott

Answer the questions. Fill in the circle beside the correct answer, or write the answer on the lines provided.

1. Who is the letter from?
   ○ Jamal   ○ Scott's mom   ○ Scott

2. Where did Scott's mom find the baseball cards?

   _____

3. In what month was the letter written?
   ○ January
   ○ February
   ○ December

Total Problems: _____   Total Correct: _____   Score: _____

Name _____   **Spot**

Read the story below.
This is Spot. Spot is a black and white dog. He likes to play fetch with Tom. Tom throws a stick. Spot runs to get the stick. Spot gives the stick to Tom. Then, they play again.

Answer the questions. Fill in the circle beside the correct answer.

1. Spot is a _____.
   ○ bird
   ○ cat
   ● dog

2. What does Spot like to do with Tom?
   ○ run
   ● fetch
   ○ dig

3. Spot is _____ and white.
   ○ brown
   ● black
   ○ blue

© Carson-Dellosa CD-2200 | Total Problems: | Total Correct: | Score: | **9**

Name _____   **Mark's New Toy**

Read the story below.
Mark saw a new toy at the store. It was a blue and red ball. Mark told his mom about the ball. His mom said, "We will get it tomorrow." After Mark got the ball, he played with it every day.

Answer the questions. Fill in the circle beside the correct answer, or write the answer on the lines provided.

1. This story is about _____.
   ● a new toy
   ○ the toy store
   ○ Mark's sister

2. The ball was blue and _____.
   ○ green
   ○ black
   ● red

3. What does Mark's mom say about the ball?

   We will get it tomorrow. _____

   _____

10 | Total Problems: | Total Correct: | Score: | © Carson-Dellosa CD-2200

Name _____   **Sam's Ball**

Read the story below.
Sam likes to play ball after school. His friends come over to his house to play. They have fun throwing and catching the ball. When it gets dark outside, his friends go home. Sam goes in the house, too.

Answer the questions. Fill in the circle beside the correct answer, or write the answer on the lines provided.

1. Write the beginning letter of each picture on the line below it.

   __c__   __h__   __k__

2. Sam likes to play _____.
   ○ video games
   ● ball
   ○ cards

3. Sam likes to play ball with _____.
   ● his friends
   ○ his mom
   ○ his dad

© Carson-Dellosa CD-2200 | Total Problems: | Total Correct: | Score: | **11**

Name _____   **Maria's Family**

Read the story below.
Maria's family is going on a trip. They have four bags to carry. The family is going to the beach. They are going to ride in a big jet. They will have fun on their trip.

Answer the questions. Fill in the circle beside the correct answer, or write the answer on the lines provided.

1. Write the beginning letter of each picture on the line below it.

   __j__et   __b__ag   __b__each

2. Maria's family is _____.
   ● going on a trip
   ○ riding on a bike
   ○ packing bags

3. Her family is going to the _____.
   ○ park
   ○ museum
   ● beach

12 | Total Problems: | Total Correct: | Score: | © Carson-Dellosa CD-2200

79

Name _____   Maria's Family

Find the words from the word box in the word search puzzle below. Circle the words you find.

Maria's Family Word Search

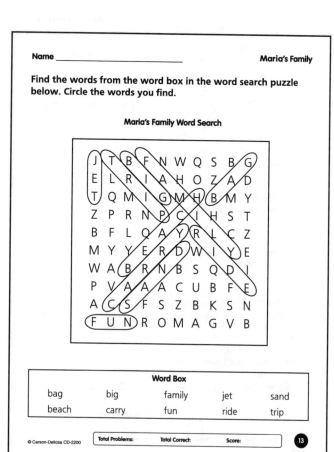

			Word Box		
bag	big	family	jet	sand
beach	carry	fun	ride	trip

Total Problems:	Total Correct:	Score:

13

Name _____   Pat's Cat

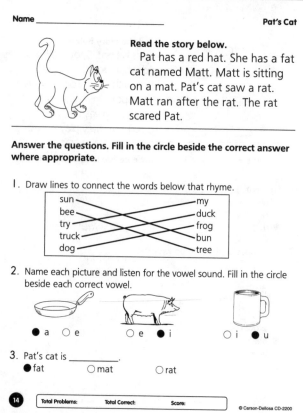

Read the story below.

Pat has a red hat. She has a fat cat named Matt. Matt is sitting on a mat. Pat's cat saw a rat. Matt ran after the rat. The rat scared Pat.

Answer the questions. Fill in the circle beside the correct answer where appropriate.

1. Draw lines to connect the words below that rhyme.

sun	my
bee	duck
try	frog
truck	bun
dog	tree

2. Name each picture and listen for the vowel sound. Fill in the circle beside each correct vowel.

● a ○ e   ○ e ● i   ○ i ● u

3. Pat's cat is _____.
   ● fat   ○ mat   ○ rat

14

Total Problems:	Total Correct:	Score:

Name _____   Long and Short Vowel Review

Circle the word that describes each picture below. Then, color the pictures.

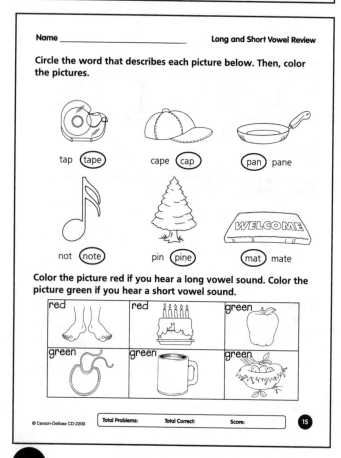

tap (tape)   cape (cap)   (pan) pane

not (note)   pin (pine)   (mat) mate

Color the picture red if you hear a long vowel sound. Color the picture green if you hear a short vowel sound.

red	red	green
green	green	green

Total Problems:	Total Correct:	Score:

15

Name _____   Mary's Flowers

Read the story below.

Mary sees some pretty flowers in the garden. She thinks her mom would like the flowers. She picks the flowers and puts them in a pretty vase. Then, she gives her mom the vase and says, "Happy Mother's Day."

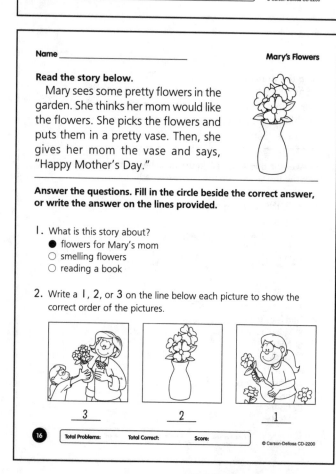

Answer the questions. Fill in the circle beside the correct answer, or write the answer on the lines provided.

1. What is this story about?
   ● flowers for Mary's mom
   ○ smelling flowers
   ○ reading a book

2. Write a 1, 2, or 3 on the line below each picture to show the correct order of the pictures.

   _3_   _2_   _1_

16

Total Problems:	Total Correct:	Score:

Worksheet 17

Name _____ Reading Sentences

Circle the sentence that tells about each picture. Color the pictures.

1. (The dog sat on the mat.)
   The mat is on the dog.
   The dog is under the mat.

2. The bus is in the garage.
   (The bus is empty.)
   The bus is full of people.

3. The cane is on the desk.
   The desk is on the cane.
   (The can is on the desk.)

© Carson-Dellosa CD-2200

Total Problems: Total Correct: Score: **17**

Worksheet 18

Name _____ Joe's Baseball Cards

18

Read the story below.

Joe loved to collect baseball cards. He loved to show his cards to all of his friends. Instead of stickers or candy, Joe wanted baseball cards. One day, he left his baseball collection on the school bus. When Joe got home, he was very sad. The bus driver gave Joe a box the next day. When Joe opened the box, his frown turned into a smile.

Answer the questions. Fill in the circle beside the correct answer where appropriate.

1. What did Joe collect?
   ○ marbles
   ○ stickers
   ● baseball cards

2. Draw a picture of where Joe left his baseball cards.

   picture should include a bus

3. What does the word "collect" mean?
   ○ to trade
   ● to gather
   ○ to play

4. What do you think was inside the box that the bus driver gave to Joe?
   ○ stickers
   ○ candy
   ● baseball cards

Total Problems: Total Correct: Score: © Carson-Dellosa CD-2200

Worksheet 19

Name _____ Janet's Butterflies

Read the story below.

Janet loves to draw pictures of butterflies. She draws pictures for her teacher, her friends, and her parents. Her butterflies have lots of colors. Janet made a book of butterflies for her mother. Her mother loved it!

Answer the questions.

1. Write a **T** on the line if the statement is true. Write an **F** if the statement is false.

   F Janet likes to draw flowers.

   T Janet uses lots of colors.

   T Her mother loved the book of butterflies.

2. Circle the words that name colors below. Put an X on the words that are not colors.

   (yellow) baXll yaXn
   frieXnd (orange) (blue)

© Carson-Dellosa CD-2200

Total Problems: Total Correct: Score: **19**

Worksheet 20

Name _____ The Soccer Game

Read the story below.

Miss Chaney's class loved to play soccer. They would play soccer every day at recess. The class would make two teams. When the game started, all of the players were ready. Sometimes the blue team would win. Sometimes the red team would win. Everyone played a good game as long as they tried their best.

Answer the questions. Fill in the circle beside the correct answer.

1. Miss Chaney's class loved to play _____.
   ○ baseball
   ● soccer
   ○ basketball

2. How many teams would the class make?
   ○ three
   ○ one
   ● two

3. Did the red team win all of the time?
   ○ yes
   ● no

4. When did Miss Chaney's class play soccer?
   ● during recess
   ○ during math
   ○ during reading

20

Total Problems: Total Correct: Score: © Carson-Dellosa CD-2200

Worksheet 21

Name _____   Long and Short Vowel Review

Circle the word that describes each picture below. Then, color the pictures.

kit (kite)   cane (can)   (tub) tube

mope (mop)   (fin) fine

Color the picture red if you hear a long vowel sound. Color the picture green if you hear a short vowel sound.

red	green	red
green	green	red

© Carson-Dellosa CD-2200   Total Problems: Total Correct: Score: **21**

Worksheet 22

Name _____   From a Seed to a Plant

Read the story below.

Seeds come in different shapes, sizes, and colors. But, all seeds have one thing in common. All seeds have tiny plants inside them. When you plant a seed in the soil and give it water and sun, a sprout will grow. A sprout is a young plant that pops out of the seed. The sprout breaks through the soil to get some sun. The leaves on the sprout soak in the sunlight. The plant uses this sunlight to make food.

Answer the questions. Fill in the circle beside the correct answer, or write the answer on the lines provided.

1. Seeds come in different shapes, sizes, and _____.
   ○ textures
   ○ tastes
   ● colors

2. How are all seeds alike?

   They have tiny plants inside them.

3. What are the three things that seeds need to grow?
   ○ water, sun, salt
   ● water, sun, soil
   ○ water, sun, shade

22   Total Problems: Total Correct: Score: © Carson-Dellosa CD-2200

Worksheet 23

Name _____   From a Seed to a Plant

Answer the questions.

4. Write a **T** on the line if the statement is true. Write an **F** if the statement is false.

   _F_   A sprout is an old plant.

   _F_   Sprouts can grow without water or sun.

   _T_   There is a tiny plant inside a seed.

   _T_   Plants make their food from sunlight.

5. Use the clues from the story to find the meanings of the words. Write the meanings on the lines below.

   sprout: _a young plant_
   that pops out of a
   seed

   soil: _dirt or ground_
   _____
   _____

6. Choose a word from the word box and write it under the picture it matches.

   Word Box
   water   sun   seeds

   sun   _seeds_   _water_

© Carson-Dellosa CD-2200   Total Problems: Total Correct: Score: **23**

Worksheet 24

Name _____   Wild Turkeys

Read the story below.

Many wild turkeys live in wooded areas of the United States. Many animals, like foxes and wolves, eat turkeys. To stay away from predators that might eat them, turkeys sleep in treetops at night. Turkeys love to eat acorns, grass, corn, and insects. They have good eyesight and hearing. Turkeys can fly for short periods of time, and they can run fast. Male turkeys are called toms, and females are called hens.

Answer the questions. Fill in the circle beside the correct answer, or write the answer on the lines provided.

1. Turkeys live in _____ areas of the United States.
   ● wooded   ○ ocean   ○ grassy

2. Female turkeys are called _____.
   ○ toms   ● hens   ○ chickens

3. Turkeys sleep in _____ at night.
   ○ water   ○ beds   ● treetops

4. Name two animals that eat turkeys. _foxes and wolves_

24   Total Problems: Total Correct: Score: © Carson-Dellosa CD-2200

Name _____ Wild Turkeys

Answer the questions.

5. Draw a picture of the four things that turkeys eat. Label each picture on the line below it.

<u>acorns</u>   <u>grass</u>   <u>corn</u>   <u>insects</u>

6. Write a **T** on the line if the statement is true. Write an **F** if the statement is false.

___F___ Chickens like to eat turkeys.

___F___ Turkeys do not run fast.

___T___ Turkeys live in wooded areas.

___T___ Turkeys can see well.

7. Use the clues from the story to find the meaning of the word. Write the meaning on the lines below.

predator: __animals that eat other animals__

_____

© Carson-Dellosa CD-2200 | Total Problems: | Total Correct: | Score: | **25**

Name _____ Paul's Trip

Read the story below.

Paul went to the zoo for his birthday. He wanted to see the bears, lions, and snakes. Paul saw the bears in their cage. He saw the lions running in the grass. But, when Paul went to see the snakes, they were hiding under the rocks. Paul was sad. "If you come back later, they will be out," the snake keeper said. Paul went back later, and he was very happy.

Answer the questions. Fill in the circle beside the correct answer.

1. Why did Paul go to the zoo?
   ○ for a field trip
   ● for his birthday
   ○ for a family trip

2. How did Paul feel when the snakes were hiding?
   ○ He was excited.
   ● He was sad.
   ○ He was angry.

3. Which animals did Paul see first?
   ○ lions   ○ snakes   ● bears

26 | Total Problems: | Total Correct: | Score: | © Carson-Dellosa CD-2200

Name _____ Paul's Trip

Find the words from the word box in the word search puzzle below. Circle the words you find.

Paul's Trip Word Search

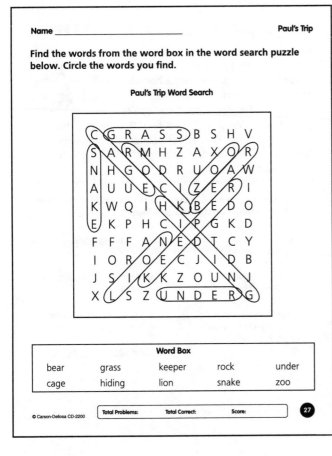

		Word Box		
bear	grass	keeper	rock	under
cage	hiding	lion	snake	zoo

© Carson-Dellosa CD-2200 | Total Problems: | Total Correct: | Score: | **27**

Name _____ Garrett Morgan 1875–1963

Read the story below.

Garrett Morgan was born in Kentucky. He invented the gas mask, which was used to help people breathe through smoke and other gases. In 1923, Garrett Morgan invented the traffic signal. The traffic signal helped cars drive safely. The traffic light we use today comes from his invention.

Answer the questions. Fill in the circle beside the correct answer, or write the answer on the lines provided.

1. Garrett Morgan was born in _____.
   ○ Alabama
   ○ Georgia
   ● Kentucky

2. How did the gas mask help people? __It helped people__ __breathe through smoke and other gases.__

3. In what year was the traffic signal invented?
   ○ 1932
   ● 1923
   ○ 1903

28 | Total Problems: | Total Correct: | Score: | © Carson-Dellosa CD-2200

Jackie Robinson 1919–1972

Name _____ Jackie Robinson 1919–1972

Read the story below.

Jackie Robinson was born in Georgia. In 1947, Robinson became the first African-American to play baseball in the Major Leagues. He played for the Brooklyn Dodgers. Robinson was a great baseball player. After he left baseball, Robinson became a businessman. In 1962, he was invited to join the Baseball Hall of Fame.

Answer the questions. Fill in the circle beside the correct answer.

1. Jackie Robinson was born in _____.
   ○ Tennessee
   ● Georgia
   ○ New York

2. Jackie Robinson was the first African-American _____ in the Major Leagues.
   ○ football player
   ○ basketball player
   ● baseball player

3. Jackie Robinson played for the Brooklyn _____.
   ● Dodgers
   ○ Braves
   ○ Yankees

4. In _____, Jackie Robinson was invited to join the Baseball Hall of Fame.
   ○ 1947
   ○ 1960
   ● 1962

© Carson-Dellosa CD-2200

Total Problems: **Total Correct:** **Score:** **29**

Marian Anderson 1902–1993

Name _____ Marian Anderson 1902–1993

Read the story below.

In 1902, Marian Anderson was born in Philadelphia, Pennsylvania. She became the first African-American singer to perform at the Metropolitan Opera House. In 1939, Eleanor Roosevelt, the wife of the president of the United States, asked Anderson to perform an outdoor concert. More than 75,000 people came to hear her sing. Marian went to Europe and learned to sing in nine different languages. In 1945, the Marian Anderson Award was formed to help other singers.

Answer the questions. Fill in the circle beside the correct answer.

1. In what year was Marian Anderson born?
   ○ 1993
   ○ 1945
   ● 1902

2. Eleanor Roosevelt asked her to sing at _____.
   ○ an indoor concert
   ● an outdoor concert
   ○ a party

3. How many languages did she learn in Europe?
   ○ six
   ○ eight
   ● nine

4. Marian Anderson was the first African-American singer to perform at:
   ● the Metropolitan Opera House
   ○ Radio City Music Hall
   ○ the White House

30 **Total Problems:** **Total Correct:** **Score:**

© Carson-Dellosa CD-2200

Thurgood Marshall 1908–1993

Name _____ Thurgood Marshall 1908–1993

Read the story below.

Thurgood Marshall was born in 1908 in Maryland. He attended Howard University, where he studied to become a lawyer. In 1952, Thurgood Marshall won the case that would eliminate, or end, school segregation. This meant that all students of any color could go to the same school. In 1967, President Johnson named Marshall to the Supreme Court of the United States. He was the first African-American Supreme Court judge.

Answer the questions. Fill in the circle beside the correct answer.

1. Thurgood Marshall was born in 1908 in _____.
   ● Maryland
   ○ Utah
   ○ Maine

2. What did Thurgood Marshall become?
   ○ a teacher
   ○ an artist
   ● a lawyer

3. In the story, what does the word "eliminate" mean?
   ○ ask
   ● end
   ○ start

© Carson-Dellosa CD-2200

Total Problems: **Total Correct:** **Score:** **31**

It's Raining

Name _____ It's Raining

Read the story below.

Jay wants to go outside to ride his new bike. He puts on his new helmet and his tennis shoes. When he gets downstairs, his mom says, "You can't go outside." "Why not?" asks Jay. "It is raining," his mom replies. Jay takes off his helmet and tennis shoes. Jay looks out the window and sighs. When the rain stops, Jay rides his bike.

Answer the questions. Fill in the circle beside the correct answer, or write the answer on the lines provided.

1. Jay wants to go outside to _____.
   ○ play ball
   ○ walk the dog
   ● ride his bike

2. What does Jay put on his head to protect himself?
   ○ his hat
   ● his helmet
   ○ his tennis shoes

3. Why does Jay sigh?
   ○ He likes the rain.
   ○ His bike is broken.
   ● He is sad because he can't go outside.

4. What do you think Jay did until it stopped raining?

   answers will vary

   _____

32 **Total Problems:** **Total Correct:** **Score:**

© Carson-Dellosa CD-2200

It's Raining

Name _____

Find the words from the word box in the word search puzzle below. Circle the words you find.

It's Raining Word Search

```
W S X M H B R N C N
I I K M O E I A F F
N G P N I M L K I X
D N O K W O E M E N
O B W G K D K J E F
W R U X I O X L Q T
N Q I S O E M F F D
Q D T L O W V U A A
J U V H E L Z T D Z
O C S N I X D J M Y
```

Word Box

bike	look	new	rain	shoe
helmet	mom	outside	sign	window

© Carson-Dellosa CD-2200

Total Problems: Total Correct: Score:

33

Keep Warm

Name _____

Read the story below.

Jessica wanted to go outside and play in the snow. Her mom said, "Bundle up! It's cold outside." So Jessica put on two sweaters. Then, she put on three pairs of pants, her mittens, her scarf, two hats, and her coat. When Jessica came downstairs, she could barely see. Her mom said, "Why do you have on all of those clothes?" "You told me to bundle up!" said Jessica.

_____

Answer the questions. Fill in the circle beside the correct answer, or write the answer on the lines provided.

1. Jessica's mom wants her to bundle up so she doesn't _____.
   ○ have fun
   ○ see anything
   ● get cold

2. Why did Jessica want to go outside? __She wanted to play__
   __in the snow._____

3. How many sweaters did Jessica put on?
   ○ five
   ● two
   ○ three

34 Total Problems: Total Correct: Score: © Carson-Dellosa CD-2200

Keep Warm

Name _____

Answer the questions.

4. Write a 1, 2, 3, 4, or 5 on each line below to show the order she put her clothes on.

   __2__ pants

   __5__ hats

   __6__ coat

   __4__ scarf

   __1__ sweaters

5. Color the hat that tells what the story was mostly about.

   Jessica wanted to build a snowman.

   Jessica had to dress warmly before she went outside.

   color

6. Choose a word from the word box and write it under the picture it matches.

Word Box

hat	scarf	mitten

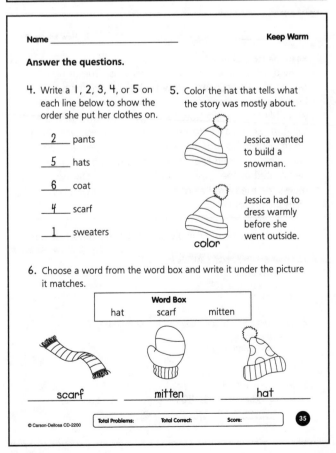

scarf   mitten   hat

© Carson-Dellosa CD-2200

Total Problems: Total Correct: Score:

35

What Time Is It?

Name _____

Read the story below.

Scott got ready for bed. He took a bath, brushed his teeth, and combed his hair. Scott was ready for a good night's sleep. Scott set his alarm clock to wake him up at seven o'clock. Scott put his head on the pillow and fell asleep quickly. When Scott's clock rang, he turned it off and went back to sleep. Scott finally woke up at nine o'clock. Scott jumped out of bed and ran to get dressed. When Scott got to school, his teacher told him he was late.

_____

Answer the questions. Fill in the circle beside the correct answer.

1. Which clock shows the time Scott wanted to get up?
   ○ eight o'clock
   ● seven o'clock
   ○ six o'clock

2. What time did school probably start?
   ○ six o'clock
   ○ nine o'clock
   ● eight o'clock

3. Scott was late to school because he _____.
   ○ missed the bus
   ○ slowly ate his breakfast
   ● overslept

36 Total Problems: Total Correct: Score: © Carson-Dellosa CD-2200

Name _____   What Time Is It?

Find the words from the word box in the word search puzzle below. Circle the words you find.

What Time Is It? Word Search

```
O  B  Q  X  G  V  Q  U  B  O
E  R  A  U  O  T  L  M  W  T
J  P  Z  T  R  X  O  O  X  B
V  J  I  S  H  C  L  K  N  C
B  V  J  P  C  L  D  Q  Y  L
R  D  Y  U  I  H  H  H  Z  O
U  X  C  P  V  O  O  A  E  C
S  S  D  M  F  V  O  O  I  K
H  E  V  N  V  X  H  O  L  R
B  A  L  A  R  M  H  J  J  Z
```

Word Box			
alarm	brush	comb	pillow
bath	clock	hair	school

© Carson-Dellosa CD-2200   Total Problems: Total Correct: Score: **37**

Name _____   Where Is Fluffy?

Read the story below.

   Lisa had a rabbit named Fluffy. She kept Fluffy in a cage in her bedroom. Lisa would feed, pet, and play with Fluffy every day after school. When Lisa got home from school one day, Fluffy was not in her cage. "Where is Fluffy?" Lisa wondered. She looked in Fluffy's favorite hiding places. First, she looked under the bed. Then, she looked in the closet. She looked in the toy chest last. Lisa couldn't find Fluffy anywhere. "Where is Fluffy?" Lisa asked aloud. Lisa's mom came into her room with Fluffy in her arms. "Fluffy is with me. I just cleaned her cage," her mom said. Lisa was happy that Fluffy was safe.

Answer the questions. Fill in the circle beside the correct answer.

1. Fluffy is Lisa's pet _____.
   ● rabbit
   ○ hamster
   ○ frog

2. Lisa feeds, pets, and _____ with Fluffy.
   ○ hops
   ● plays
   ○ eats

3. Lisa was _____ when she couldn't find Fluffy.
   ● worried
   ○ angry
   ○ confused

4. What did Lisa ask when she didn't see Fluffy in the cage?
   ○ "Where is my rabbit?"
   ○ "Who has Fluffy?"
   ● "Where is Fluffy?"

38   Total Problems: Total Correct: Score: © Carson-Dellosa CD-2200

Name _____   Where Is Fluffy?

Answer the questions.

5. Write a **1**, **2**, or **3** on the line below each picture to show the order that Lisa looked for Fluffy.

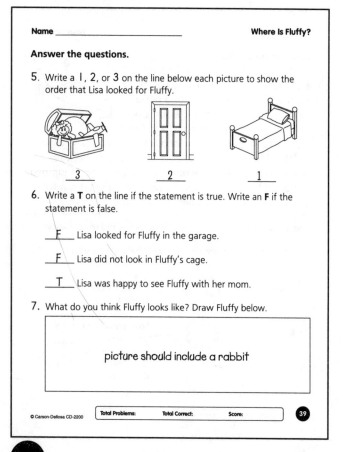

   ___3___   ___2___   ___1___

6. Write a **T** on the line if the statement is true. Write an **F** if the statement is false.

   __F__ Lisa looked for Fluffy in the garage.

   __F__ Lisa did not look in Fluffy's cage.

   __T__ Lisa was happy to see Fluffy with her mom.

7. What do you think Fluffy looks like? Draw Fluffy below.

   picture should include a rabbit

© Carson-Dellosa CD-2200   Total Problems: Total Correct: Score: **39**

Name _____   How Tall Am I?

Read the story below.

   Reid always asked his mom questions. One of his favorite questions was, "How tall am I?" So, for his birthday, Reid's mom got him a measuring tape. Reid was able to measure how tall he was. He was 48 inches tall. But, Reid didn't stop there. He measured everything. He measured his arm, his ear, his leg, his foot, and his hair. One day, Reid took his measuring tape to school. He wanted to see how tall his friends were. During recess, he measured all of his friends. Reid loved his birthday present!

Answer the questions. Fill in the circle beside the correct answer.

1. What did Reid always ask his mother?
   ○ "How big am I?"
   ○ "How short am I?"
   ● "How tall am I?"

2. What did Reid's mother buy him for his birthday?
   ○ a ruler
   ● a measuring tape
   ○ stickers

3. How tall was Reid?
   ● 48 inches   ○ 40 inches   ○ 63 inches

40   Total Problems: Total Correct: Score: © Carson-Dellosa CD-2200

Name _____   How Tall Am I?

Find the words from the word box in the word search puzzle below. Circle the words you find.

How Tall Am I? Word Search

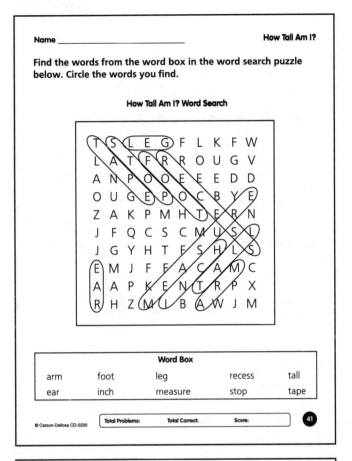

Word Box				
arm	foot	leg	recess	tall
ear	inch	measure	stop	tape

© Carson-Dellosa CD-2200 — Total Problems: — Total Correct: — Score: — **41**

Name _____   Safety Rules

Read the story below.

On Monday, Miss Smith's class talked about safety. Each student gave a safety tip to the class. Alex said, "You should wear a helmet when you ride your bike." Sarah said, "You should wear a life jacket when you are in a boat." "If you play football, you should wear a helmet and shoulder pads," said Joe. After they finished talking about safety, the class cut out pictures of their safety tips.

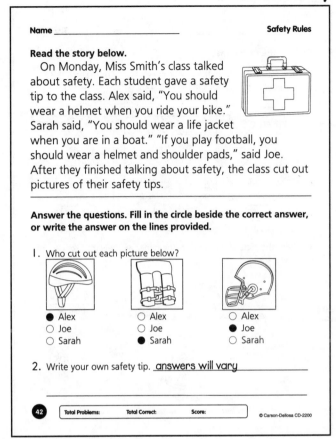

Answer the questions. Fill in the circle beside the correct answer, or write the answer on the lines provided.

1. Who cut out each picture below?

   ● Alex   ○ Alex   ○ Alex
   ○ Joe   ○ Joe   ● Joe
   ○ Sarah   ● Sarah   ○ Sarah

2. Write your own safety tip. **answers will vary** _____

42 — Total Problems: — Total Correct: — Score: — © Carson-Dellosa CD-2200

Name _____   Safety Rules

Find the words from the word box in the word search puzzle below. Circle the words you find.

Safety Rules Word Search

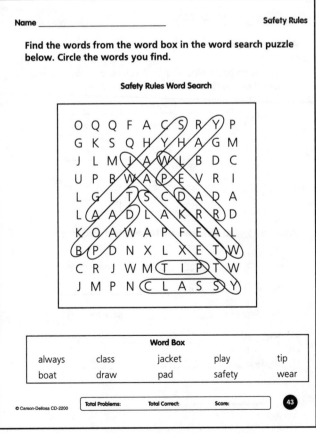

Word Box				
always	class	jacket	play	tip
boat	draw	pad	safety	wear

© Carson-Dellosa CD-2200 — Total Problems: — Total Correct: — Score: — **43**

Name _____   The Weed

Read the story below.

The Layton family loved to plant in their garden. Everyone pitched in to help. One day, Mr. Layton tried to pull a weed out of the ground. He pulled and pulled, but it didn't come out. So, he asked his wife to help. They pulled, but it didn't come out. So, they asked their children to help. They pulled and pulled, but the weed did not come out. Then, their dog Spot saw them pulling and wanted to help. He grabbed the weed with his teeth and pulled. The weed finally came out, and the family cheered!

Answer the questions. Fill in the circle beside the correct answer.

1. What did the family like to do?
   ● plant in the garden
   ○ wash the car
   ○ walk the dog

2. Who helped Mr. Layton first?
   ○ his children
   ○ the dog
   ● his wife

3. What did the family try to get out of the ground?
   ● a weed
   ○ a flower
   ○ a bug

4. Who helped last?
   ○ the father
   ● the dog
   ○ the children

44 — Total Problems: — Total Correct: — Score: — © Carson-Dellosa CD-2200

Name _____ The Weed

Answer the questions.

5. Write a 1, 2, or 3 in the box below each picture to show the correct order in which the family helped.

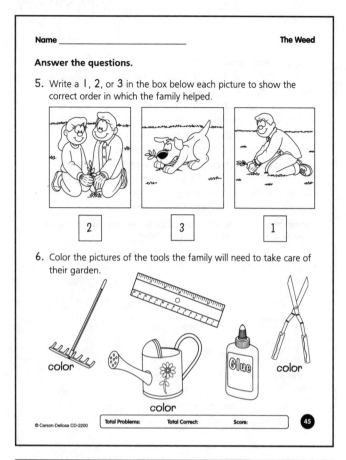

2   3   1

6. Color the pictures of the tools the family will need to take care of their garden.

color   color

color

© Carson-Dellosa CD-2200 | Total Problems: | Total Correct: | Score: | 45

Name _____ Tim's Golf Ball

Read the story below.

Tim loves golf. His parents bought him golf clubs and a box of golf balls. Instead of cartoons, Tim watches golf on television. He practices golf in his backyard every day after school. He takes his golf clubs and balls outside. He sets the ball on the golf tee. Then, he swings the golf club and hits the ball. One day, the ball went sailing through the air into his neighbor's yard. Tim heard a loud noise and became worried. Then, Tim's mom came outside and asked what the sound was.

Answer the questions. Fill in the circle beside the correct answer.

1. Tim likes to play _____.
   ○ basketball
   ○ soccer
   ● golf

2. Tim's parents bought him _____.
   ● golf clubs and balls
   ○ a baseball
   ○ a football

3. What do you think happened?
   ○ Tim's golf club broke.
   ○ Tim's golf ball cracked.
   ● Tim broke his neighbor's window.

4. How does Tim feel?
   ○ happy
   ○ mad
   ● worried

46 | Total Problems: | Total Correct: | Score: | © Carson-Dellosa CD-2200

Name _____ Anita's Messy Room

Read the story below.

Anita has to clean her room once a week. Her room was very messy today! Anita started to hang her clothes in the closet and put her toys in the toy chest. Then, Anita noticed it was one o'clock. It was time for her favorite television show. Anita had not finished cleaning, so she pushed the rest of the toys under the bed. Anita ran downstairs and turned on the television. "Did you finish cleaning your room, Anita?" her mom asked. "Not exactly," Anita said. Anita knew she had to turn off the television and go upstairs.

Answer the questions. Fill in the circle beside the correct answer.

1. Anita cleans her room _____.
   ○ every day
   ○ every Monday
   ● once a week

2. Anita started to hang her clothes in the _____.
   ○ chest
   ● closet
   ○ bathroom

© Carson-Dellosa CD-2200 | Total Problems: | Total Correct: | Score: | 47

Name _____ Classifying by Color

Answer the questions.

1. In the word box, color the squares with the color words orange. Color the verbs blue. Color the number words yellow. Color the nouns green.

Word Box

orange white	blue jump	yellow two
green dog	orange black	green teacher
blue hop	green car	orange blue
yellow one	blue run	orange green

2. Choose a word from the word box that best completes each sentence. Write the words on the lines provided.

The _car_ drove down the street.

The rabbit likes to _hop_.

The _teacher_ gave the class homework.

I have _two_ ears.

The sky is _blue_.

48 | Total Problems: | Total Correct: | Score: | © Carson-Dellosa CD-2200

Name _____   Reading Sentences

Circle the sentence that tells about each picture. Color the pictures.

1. The cloud is over the city.
   The plow is in the field.
   (The clown is in the park.)

2. The girl plays with a top.
   (The girl plays with a doll.)
   The girl plays on a team.

3. (Judy walks to school.)
   Judy runs to the bus stop.
   Judy rides to the store.

| Total Problems: | Total Correct: | Score: | **49** |

© Carson-Dellosa CD-2200

Name _____   A Friend Like Jessica

Read the story below.

Lindsey and Jessica were best friends. They did everything together. One day, Jessica's parents told her that they were going to move. Jessica was very upset. When she told Lindsey, Lindsey was sad. "Who will be my best friend now?" Lindsey asked. Jessica said, "I will. We can still write and visit each other." When Jessica moved away, the girls kept in touch like they had promised.

Answer the questions. Fill in the circle beside the correct answer, or write the answer on the lines provided.

1. The girls were _____.
   ○ enemies
   ○ sisters
   ● best friends

2. How did Jessica feel when her parents told her they were going to move?
   ○ happy
   ● upset
   ○ excited

3. What would be a good title for this story?
   ○ Getting a New Friend
   ○ Moving
   ● My Friend Moved Away

4. How would you feel if you were Lindsey?

   _____ answers will vary _____

   _____

   _____

| **50** | Total Problems: | Total Correct: | Score: | © Carson-Dellosa CD-2200 |

Name _____   A Friend Like Jessica

Find the words from the word box in the word search puzzle below. Circle the words you find.

A Friend Like Jessica Word Search

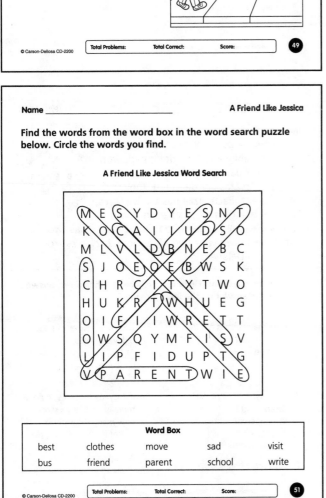

Word Box				
best	clothes	move	sad	visit
bus	friend	parent	school	write

| Total Problems: | Total Correct: | Score: | **51** |

© Carson-Dellosa CD-2200

Name _____   Linda's Cookies

Read the story below.

Linda and Mom love to bake. They bake cakes and brownies. But, their favorite thing to bake is cookies. First, Linda takes out the flour, milk, eggs, and chocolate chips. She mixes the dough in a bowl. She makes little balls with the dough and places them on the cookie sheet. Then, Linda's mom puts the cookies into the oven while Linda finishes her homework. "What is that smell?" Mom suddenly asks. "Oh, my cookies!" yells Linda. Linda runs into the kitchen and opens the oven.

Answer the questions. Fill in the circle beside the correct answer.

1. What do Linda and her mom love to bake?
   ○ pies
   ● cookies
   ○ bread

2. Which ingredient did Linda not use to make her cookies?
   ○ eggs
   ○ flour
   ● apples

3. What do you think happened to their cookies?
   ● They burned.
   ○ They were too small.
   ○ They tasted good.

4. What would be a good title for this story?
   ○ The Good Cookies
   ● The Burned Cookies
   ○ The Good Cake

| **52** | Total Problems: | Total Correct: | Score: | © Carson-Dellosa CD-2200 |

Linda's Cookies

Name _____

Answer the questions.

5. Describe how you think Linda's cookies could have been saved.

   __answers will vary_____

   _____

   _____

   _____

   _____

6. What caused Linda's cookies to burn in the oven?
   ● She was doing her homework.
   ○ She didn't turn on the oven.
   ○ She fell asleep.

7. Draw a picture of what you think Linda's cookies looked like when she opened the oven.

   pictures will vary

© Carson-Dellosa CD-2200 | Total Problems: Total Correct: Score: **53**

The Jack-o'-Lantern Contest

Name _____

Read the story below.

   Ms. Proctor's class had a jack-o'lantern contest. The student who could carve the best pumpkin would win a trip to the candy store. Everyone brought in pumpkins. Joe and Scott both wanted to win the contest. First, they drew the faces on their pumpkins. Then, they each cut out eyes, a nose, and a mouth. Each boy knew he had to do his best if he was going to win. The next day, the principal came into the class to judge. He thought Joe's and Scott's pumpkins were great. But, the principal could only pick one. The principal said, "The winner is. . ."

Answer the questions. Write the answers on the lines provided.

1. Ms. Proctor's class decided to have a __jack-o'-lantern contest__.

2. What would the winner of the contest get?

   __a trip to the candy store_____

3. The __principal_____ judged the contest.

4. Scott and Joe knew they had to do their __best_____ if they wanted to win.

54 Total Problems: Total Correct: Score: © Carson-Dellosa CD-2200

The Jack-o'-Lantern Contest

Name _____

Answer the questions.

5. Follow the directions below to make Joe's and Scott's jack-o'-lanterns.

   Scott   **Joe**

   pictures will vary   pictures will vary

   Draw two triangles for the eyes.   Draw two circles for the eyes.
   Draw one square for the nose.   Draw one rectangle for the nose.
   Draw a smiling mouth with two teeth.   Draw a frowning mouth with five teeth.
   Color the pumpkin orange.   Color the pumpkin orange.
   Color the stem green.   Color the stem green.

6. Who do you think won the contest? Color the ribbon blue for the person you think should win the contest.

   Scott   answers will vary   **Joe**

© Carson-Dellosa CD-2200 | Total Problems: Total Correct: Score: **55**

Pizza Night

Name _____

Read the story below.

   Tonight is pizza night at the Marion house. Delaney and Troy get a pepperoni pizza. Their parents get a cheese pizza. When the pizzas are delivered, they sit down to eat. Each pizza has twelve slices. So, everyone gets six slices each. Mom and Dad eat all of their pizza. But, Delaney has two slices left. "May I have your two slices of pizza?" asks Troy. "Yes," says Delaney.

Answer the questions. Fill in the circle beside the correct answer, or write the answer on the lines provided.

1. How many pizzas did the family order?
   ○ three
   ● two
   ○ four

2. What type of pizza did Delaney eat?
   ● pepperoni
   ○ cheese
   ○ mushroom

3. Each pizza had __twelve__ slices.

4. How many slices of pizza did Mom eat?
   ○ ten
   ○ twelve
   ● six

5. If Troy ate his slices of pizza, then ate Delaney's slices, how many slices of pizza did he eat in all?
   ○ ten
   ● eight
   ○ six

56 Total Problems: Total Correct: Score: © Carson-Dellosa CD-2200

Name _____   Pizza Night

Find the words from the word box in the word search puzzle below. Circle the words you find.

Pizza Night Word Search

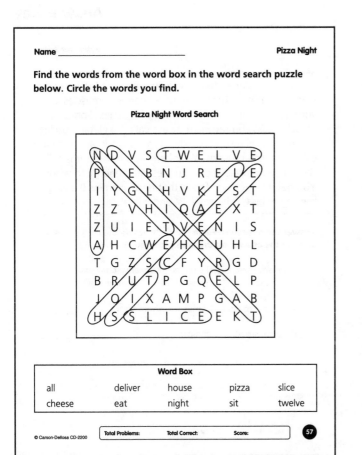

				Word Box			
all		deliver	house		pizza		slice
cheese		eat	night		sit		twelve

© Carson-Dellosa CD-2200   Total Problems: Total Correct: Score: **57**

Name _____   Julie's Doll

Read the story below.

  Julie loves to dress and feed her doll, Betty. She even has tea parties with Betty. Julie's brother James likes to play tricks on Julie. One day, James hid Julie's doll. "Have you seen Betty?" Julie asked. "No," said James. Then, Julie looked in the closet and found Betty. James started laughing.

Answer the questions. Fill in the circle beside the correct answer.

1. What does Julie enjoy doing with Betty?
   ○ dressing and walking her
   ○ feeding and walking her
   ● dressing and feeding her

2. What did James do after Julie found her doll in the closet?
   ○ He ran away.
   ○ He hid another doll.
   ● He started to laugh.

3. Do you think James will hide Julie's doll again? Why or why not?

   __answers will vary_____

   _____

58   Total Problems: Total Correct: Score: © Carson-Dellosa CD-2200

Name _____   Reading Sentences

Circle the sentence that tells about each picture. Color the pictures.

1. His mitten did not fit.
   (William sits on the rug.)
   I can fix the fan.

3. Dan will hit the ball.
   Dan will hit the bat.
   (Jan washes the car.)

2. I will run to get the cab.
   (Hank is wearing a new cap.)
   Jill was in the cab.

4. (Katrina counts the coins.)
   Katrina runs the bases.
   Katrina walks to school.

© Carson-Dellosa CD-2200   Total Problems: Total Correct: Score: **59**

Name _____   The Skeletal System

Read the story below.

  Your body is made up of many systems. Your bones are part of your skeletal system. Your body is made up of 206 bones. Bones give your body its shape. If you did not have a skeleton, you would look like a rag doll. Your bones are hard and help you stand and sit. Vitamin D keeps your bones and teeth strong and healthy. Vitamin D is found in foods like milk and fish.

Answer the questions. Fill in the circle beside the correct answer, or write the answer on the lines provided.

1. Your body is made up of

   ___206___ bones.

2. Bones give your body its

   ___shape___.

3. Your bones make up your

   _____.
   ○ bone system
   ● skeletal system
   ○ strong system

4. Your bones are _____.
   ○ soft
   ○ rubber
   ● hard

5. Which vitamin helps to keep your bones and teeth healthy?
   ○ vitamin A
   ○ vitamin C
   ● vitamin D

60   Total Problems: Total Correct: Score: © Carson-Dellosa CD-2200

Name _____   The Skeletal System

Find the words from the word box in the word search puzzle below. Circle the words you find.

The Skeletal System Word Search

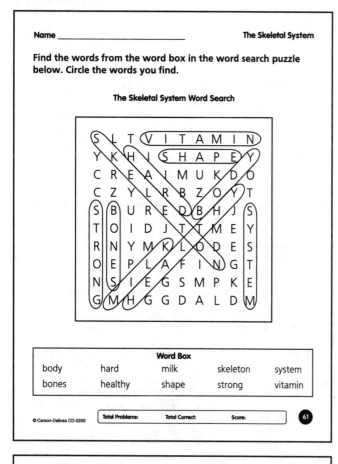

Word Box

body	hard	milk	skeleton	system
bones	healthy	shape	strong	vitamin

© Carson-Dellosa CD-2200 · Total Problems: · Total Correct: · Score: · **61**

Name _____   The Muscular System

Read the story below.

Your muscular system is very important. Muscles make your body move. There are more than 650 muscles in your body. There are three types of muscles. Some muscles help you move. They are called skeletal muscles. Some muscles help your other organs work, and they are called smooth muscles. Your heart is a muscle. It is called the cardiac muscle. Your muscles need energy to work. You get energy from foods that have vitamins B and D, like vegetables, fish, peanuts, and wheat.

Answer the questions. Fill in the circle beside the correct answer, or write the answer on the lines provided.

1. How many muscles make up the muscular system?
   ○ over 206   ○ over 700   ● over 650

2. Name the three types of muscles in your body.

   skeletal, smooth, cardiac

   _____

3. Your muscles need _____ to work.
   ● energy   ○ bones   ○ water

62 · Total Problems: · Total Correct: · Score: · © Carson-Dellosa CD-2200

Name _____   The Muscular System

Find the words from the word box in the word search puzzle below. Circle the words you find

The Muscular System Word Search

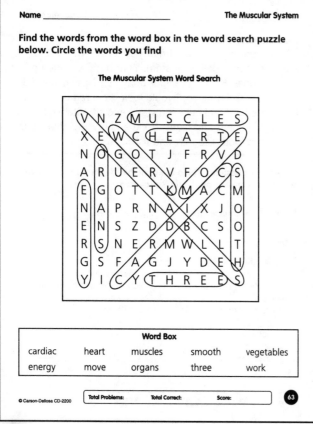

Word Box

cardiac	heart	muscles	smooth	vegetables
energy	move	organs	three	work

© Carson-Dellosa CD-2200 · Total Problems: · Total Correct: · Score: · **63**

Name _____   The Digestive System

Read the story below.

Your digestive system starts to work as soon as you put food in your mouth. Your mouth chews and breaks down the food. Saliva mixes with the food to make it easier to swallow. When you swallow, the food travels from your esophagus to your stomach. Your stomach turns the food into a thick soup. Then, it travels to your small intestine. Your small intestine takes out vitamins and minerals and sends them to your blood. The rest of the food travels to your large intestine, where most of the water is taken out. The rest leaves your body as waste. It takes three days for food to go through your entire digestive system.

Answer the questions. Write the answers on the lines provided.

1. The digestive system starts in your _mouth_.

2. What mixes with food to make it easier for you to swallow?

   saliva

3. What does your stomach do? _turns the food into a thick soup_

4. The small intestine takes out _vitamins_ and _minerals_.

64 · Total Problems: · Total Correct: · Score: · © Carson-Dellosa CD-2200

Name _____   The Digestive System

Find the words from the word box in the word search puzzle below. Circle the words you find.

The Digestive System Word Search

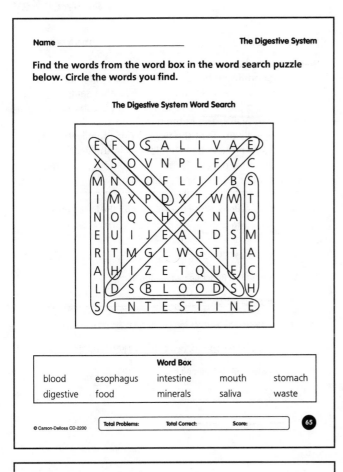

Word Box				
blood	esophagus	intestine	mouth	stomach
digestive	food	minerals	saliva	waste

© Carson-Dellosa CD-2200 | Total Problems: | Total Correct: | Score: | **65**

Name _____   Pond Life

Read the story below.

A pond is an area of fresh, still water. It can be made by nature or by man. Many different plants, insects, and animals live in a pond. Pond plants are very important. They provide homes, food, and hiding places for many animals. They also keep the pond healthy. All of the things that live in or near the pond are linked together. The algae that grows in the pond is eaten by tadpoles. Tadpoles are eaten by baby turtles. Baby turtles are eaten by frogs. Frogs are eaten by fish, and fish are eaten by herons.

Answer the questions. Write the answers on the lines provided.

1. What is a pond? _an area of fresh, still water_____

_____

2. How can a pond be made? _by nature or by man_____

_____

3. How do insects and animals depend on pond plants?

_They provide homes, food, hiding places, and keep__

_the pond healthy._____

66 | Total Problems: | Total Correct: | Score: | © Carson-Dellosa CD-2200

Name _____   Pond Life

Answer the questions.

4. Write a **1**, **2**, **3**, **4**, **5**, or **6** on the line below each picture in the order that the plants and animals are linked together.

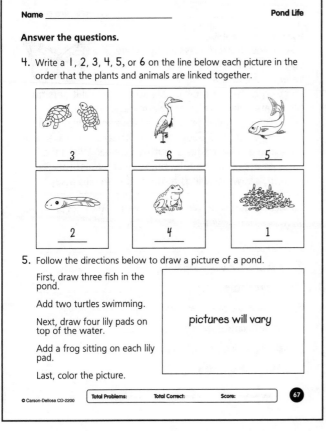

5. Follow the directions below to draw a picture of a pond.

First, draw three fish in the pond.

Add two turtles swimming.

Next, draw four lily pads on top of the water.

Add a frog sitting on each lily pad.

Last, color the picture.

pictures will vary

© Carson-Dellosa CD-2200 | Total Problems: | Total Correct: | Score: | **67**

Name _____   Contraction Action

Answer the questions.

1. Draw a line from each contraction in the left column to the words in the right column that form it.

didn't		can not
isn't		have not
wasn't		are not
can't		is not
weren't		could not
aren't		did not
haven't		was not
couldn't		were not

2. Study the underlined contraction in each sentence. Write the words that form the contraction on the lines provided.

I'll go to the store. _I will_____

She hasn't finished her lunch. _has not_____

Jenny won't leave yet. _will not_____

You shouldn't run. _should not_____

We're hungry. _We are_____

68 | Total Problems: | Total Correct: | Score: | © Carson-Dellosa CD-2200

Worksheet 1 (top left)

Name _____ More Contraction Action

Circle the word that best completes each sentence. Write the word on the line provided.

1. _____She's_____ going to the store. — She'll / (She's)
2. _____I've_____ eaten all of the pizza. — (I've) / I'm
3. _____That's_____ my favorite picture. — Let's / (That's)
4. _____He's_____ my best friend. — He'll / (He's)
5. _____They'll_____ be back soon. — (They'll) / They've
6. Brandon __isn't__ washing the car. — (isn't) / didn't
7. Mom __shouldn't__ be late for dinner. — aren't / (shouldn't)
8. Dad __didn't__ win the race. — wasn't / (didn't)

© Carson-Dellosa CD-2200 — Total Problems: — Total Correct: — Score: — **69**

Worksheet 2 (top right)

Name _____ Tim's New Puppy

Read the story below.

Tim's friend Roger has a puppy named Spot. One day, Tim asked his parents for a puppy. His father said, "A puppy is a big job. You have to feed him, brush him, take him for walks, and bathe him." Tim said, "If you get me a puppy, I'll do all of the work." Tim's family went to the pet store the next day. Tim looked in the window and picked out a puppy. "What are you going to name him?" his mom asked. "Spot," said Tim.

Answer the questions. Write the answers on the lines provided.

1. Why do you think Tim wanted a puppy?
   answers will vary
2. Why do you think Roger named his dog Spot?
   answers will vary
3. When Tim asked his parents for a dog, what did his dad say?
   Puppies need to be fed, brushed, walked, and bathed.
4. Why do you think Tim named his dog Spot?
   answers will vary

70 — Total Problems: — Total Correct: — Score: — © Carson-Dellosa CD-2200

Worksheet 3 (bottom left)

Name _____ Tim's New Puppy

Find the words from the word box in the word search puzzle below. Circle the words you find.

Tim's New Puppy Word Search

```
L R W H I T E K P P
A H L Y E M L M S U
C R Z F F A U X T P
Q A F O W J M Q O P
Y B R S K Q O D R Y
C O R C P Q V R E M
E K A U F O B Y C G
W L V B S E T O K Q
B O W K L H E R I K
G H H R L Q M D P C
```

Word Box

| black | car | jump | spot | walk |
| brush | feed | puppy | store | white |

© Carson-Dellosa CD-2200 — Total Problems: — Total Correct: — Score: — **71**

Worksheet 4 (bottom right)

Name _____ From a Caterpillar to a Butterfly

Read the story below.

A mother butterfly lays a tiny, white egg on a leaf. The egg pops open two weeks later, and a small caterpillar comes out. The caterpillar eats and eats until it gets fat. Most caterpillars like to eat plant leaves and grasses. Then, the caterpillar finds a safe place and builds a silky covering around its body called a chrysalis. The caterpillar stays in the chrysalis for about two weeks. When the chrysalis opens, a beautiful butterfly emerges. The butterfly allows its wings to dry and then flies away.

Answer the questions. Write the answers on the lines provided.

1. Where does the mother butterfly place her egg?
   on a leaf
2. What pops out of the egg?
   a small caterpillar
3. What does the caterpillar do when it pops out of the egg?
   it eats until it gets fat
4. Name two things that a caterpillar eats.
   leaves and grass

72 — Total Problems: — Total Correct: — Score: — © Carson-Dellosa CD-2200

Name _____   From a Caterpillar to a Butterfly

Find the words from the word box in the word search puzzle below. Circle the words you find.

From a Caterpillar to a Butterfly Word Search

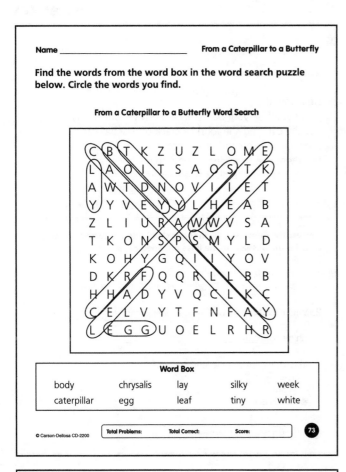

Word Box				
body	chrysalis	lay	silky	week
caterpillar	egg	leaf	tiny	white

© Carson-Dellosa CD-2200   Total Problems: Total Correct: Score: **73**

Name _____   Reading Sentences

Circle the sentence that tells about each picture. Color the pictures.

1. (The tag is on the bag.)
   The cat is on the mat.
   The man is in the van.

3. (Dan has a big dog.)
   Erin is sad.
   The pot is hot.

2. (Her dad has a cane.)
   Liz is wearing a cape.
   Pat hit the ball with a bat.

4. The fox is in the log.
   (Irene mops the floor.)
   Joey sat in the red chair.

74   Total Problems: Total Correct: Score: © Carson-Dellosa CD-2200

Name _____   Dear Jane

Read the letter below.

November 29, 2003

Dear Jane,

   I am glad that you came from Florida to visit me. I had a lot of fun playing with our dolls and other toys. I liked playing ball in my backyard. I had a great time when we made cookies together. I hope we can see each other again soon. Maybe I can visit you in Florida next time. I hope you had a good time, too.

            Love,
            Jill

Answer the questions. Fill in the circle beside the correct answer, or write the answer on the lines provided.

1. Who wrote the letter?
   ○ Jane   ● Jill   ○ Florida

2. Name two things that the girls did together. **played with their dolls, played ball, made cookies**

3. Where does Jane live? **Florida**

4. When was the letter written?
   ○ November 12   ○ November 10   ● November 29

© Carson-Dellosa CD-2200   Total Problems: Total Correct: Score: **75**

Name _____   Dear Joe

Read the letter below.

June 16, 2001

Dear Joe,

   Can you go fishing with me? I have asked five other classmates to come. We will be leaving from my house on Saturday morning at four o'clock. My dad says we have to be awake before the fish. We will bait our hooks and catch as many fish as we can. Please come!

            Your friend,
            Alex

Answer the questions. Fill in the circle beside the correct answer, or write the answer on the lines provided.

1. What are they going to do on the boat? **go fishing**

2. How many classmates can Alex invite in all? **six**

3. In what month was the letter written?
   ○ July
   ○ January
   ● June

4. What time are they leaving Alex's house? **four o'clock**

76   Total Problems: Total Correct: Score: © Carson-Dellosa CD-2200

Name _____   **Dear Uncle Charles**

Read the letter below.

September 13, 2010

Dear Uncle Charles,

   It is the beginning of school. I am in the first grade this year. My teacher says we will learn a lot of new things, like how to read, write, add, and subtract. The best thing about first grade is we will go on field trips! We are going to the museum in December. My teacher said we can bring someone with us. Could you go with me? I hope you can!

Love,
Anne

Answer the questions. Fill in the circle beside the correct answer, or write the answer on the lines provided.

1. Who is the letter for?
   ○ the teacher   ○ Anne   ● Uncle Charles

2. What grade is Anne in? _first_____

3. Name two things Anne will learn in first grade. _reading,_____

   _writing, adding, subtracting_____

© Carson-Dellosa CD-2200 | Total Problems: | Total Correct: | Score: | **77**

Name _____   **Dear Jamal**

Read the letter below.

December 5, 2005

Dear Jamal,

   Did you lose your baseball cards? My mom was cleaning out the car, and she found a stack of baseball cards. You probably left them after our scout meeting yesterday. I put them in a box. Please come to my house and look through them. I think they are yours.

Thanks,
Scott

Answer the questions. Fill in the circle beside the correct answer, or write the answer on the lines provided.

1. Who is the letter from?
   ○ Jamal   ○ Scott's mom   ● Scott

2. Where did Scott's mom find the baseball cards?

   _in her car_____

3. In what month was the letter written?
   ○ January
   ○ February
   ● December

78 | Total Problems: | Total Correct: | Score: | © Carson-Dellosa CD-2200